SEAGULLS ON SPEED
© 2012 by Graeme Scarfe.

The book author retains sole copyright to his contributions to this book.

First imprint: 2013; Second imprint 2017

Cover illustration by Dave Exton

The Blurb-provided layout designs and graphic elements are copyright Blurb Inc. This book was created using the Blurb creative publishing service. The book author retains sole copyright to his or her contributions to this book.

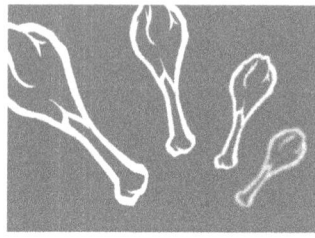

SEAGULLS ON SPEED

Graeme Scarfe
© 2013

About the author:

Graeme Scarfe was born in the 1960's, educated in the comprehensive system in the 1970's & 1980's and graduated from Bournemouth University in the 1990's. At various times he has worked as a music journalist, sound recordist, stand-up comedian and teacher of film and media.

A member of the Writers' Guild of Great Britain, and represented by The Tennyson Agency, he is married with two children and lives in Sussex.

Other books by the same author include *Arable Farm*, a children's novel for 8+ years, also available from Blurb.co.uk

No seagulls or sea-birds of any description were eaten during the writing of this book.

Dedicated to:
Rachel, Thom & Niamh.

1

From whichever way you looked at it Folkestone represented the end. From London, it was the final point on the map before your train went underground and onto the continent. From mainland Europe it was the end of the Eurozone, the high-speed rail links and the good food.

For Gasmark it was a lobster pot. After a brief spell at Catering College in Kettering he had decided the only way to learn about food was to spend time in the melting pots of Haute Cuisine which, in his fevered imagination meant only one thing: the great kitchens of Paris. So he had arrived in Folkestone en-route to his destiny with a pocket-sized *Rough Guide to France* in his rucksack along with some cookery books – Delia (of course), a tattered copy of '*The Galloping Gourmet*' by Graham Kerr and a couple of Jamie Oliver's plus a handful of self-created recipes which he believed showed his potential and the set of *Sabatier* knives secretly 'liberated' from the kitchens of the College he had recently departed.

Folkestone was to be the last stop before the big push. The Great Leap Forwards.

The final grand meal on Blighty before he set sail for the continent. Like the banquets enjoyed by the generals before Waterloo. That was the plan, and like all great plans it was scuppered by fate. A chance meeting with a couple of friendly girls in a seafront nightclub had led to what he thought was going to be a good time. But when he woke up face down in the sand hours later, with what he suspected was a Rohypnol hangover, he discovered he'd lost more than just his dignity. Gone was his wallet, his money, his ferry ticket and, more importantly, his European dream.

So instead of being the beginning Folkestone was, for Gasmark, very much the end. Or at least the beginning of the end, because the longer he remained in the town, with its tantalizing views of Calais on a clear day, the more it began to feel like his dream was deflating like a ruined soufflé. The realisation that Brexit Britain was just an isolationist dead-end only reinforced the feeling that Britain wasn't so Great after all.

One McJob led to another and another until he finally managed to talk his way into a kitchen. Well, not so much a kitchen in the static sense, but in the portable sense. He was head chef in a mobile burger van. Only yet again life was cruel. The local businessman who had spotted Gasmark's culinary potential had, in actual fact, spotted his desperation, and Head Chef actually meant *Only Chef* and included pretty much everything else too. His only consolation was Sally, the Business graduate who worked the till, made the tea, provided the conversation and kept him sane.

Leaning on the counter he looked out across the English Channel towards the thin grey line on the horizon that was France and wondered, not for the first time, if there was a disillusioned French Anglophile wanna-be chef who wanted nothing more than to work in the kitchens of London, but was stuck in a fast-food van flipping burgers for the guards who worked at Sangatte gazing back across that thin stretch of water.

The piercing cry of a seagull snapped him out of his reverie. For a brief moment he watched the sea-bird peck at some leftover that had been discarded by one of his more discerning customers before slapping his hand on the counter and frightening the bird off in a great flap of wings.

"Bloody things," he said to no one in particular.

The smell, the sweet, delicious, guilty smell of onions frying on a hotplate was the key. It wafted hither and thither from the cliff top by the Martello tower and called, like sirens to the faintly hungry. On a good day, with an obliging wind, Gasmark liked to think that the smell of his onions even made it to France.

But whatever the geographical stretch of the aroma, more closely to home it always brought forth customers. Happy roadside gastronomes for whom the simple burger in a bun topped with oily fried onions that had been sprinkled with sugar to caramelize for an instant never failed to be grateful for the feast in a paper napkin that Gasmark brought forth and handed over. If nothing else in his life, he liked to think that he was at least succeeding on one level: fulfilling a basic need.

Of course self-delusion counts for a lot.

"Whaddya call that?" asked the slightly overweight man in dirty jeans and a fading *Empire Strikes Back* T-Shirt straining over his belly. Gasmark looked up from behind the counter to regard the customer properly for the first time.

"A burger," he replied.

The Empire shook his head holding the thin bap, limp lettuce and sliver of burger so to give the best impression of something that had long ago given up the ghost.

"You're having a laugh," he said, slapping the offending offering back down on the counter,

"I'm not paying for that."

Gasmark regarded the pathetic excuse for a burger and realised the awful truth. Slowly, and without disagreement, he reached across to the till, opened it, scooped up the coins that had only just been dropped in and handed them back.

The Empire had struck back and won.

The retreating figure wobbled away, counting the change in his paw with stubby, sausage-like fingers and all Gasmark could do was watch and reflect on the depressing metaphor the dissatisfied customer represented for his hopes and dreams.

With plummeting spirits he picked up the burger between his thumb and forefinger and tossed it out of the van whereupon it was immediately swooped upon by three hungry seagulls for whom there was always such a thing as a free lunch.

2

Across town, tucked away apologetically behind the buildings that made up Folkestone's town centre sat a church and its graveyard that was hardly ever troubled by parishioners. The Sunday services were so poorly attended that these days even the vicar was selective in his attendance.

But today, as the early summer day struggled to put in a really good, hot appearance there was an air of activity in the building. Someone had died, and that was always guaranteed pew filler.

At one hundred and three, Harold Hedley Hegley-Stone had out-lived a lot of his closest relatives but he had still been popular enough in the town to stimulate the church numbers and today the Right Reverend Peter Goose was expecting a full house. "Might even be standing room only!" he'd chuckled to himself walking up the path towards the church doors earlier, and then crossed himself for fear of appearing too happy on such an occasion. But he had good reason to be happy, because a funeral - and a particularly well attended one as todays promised to be - always paid dividends when it came time for the collection bowl to do the rounds. Today he was expecting a tidy sum, and the Lord had pointed him in the direction of the 4.30 at Chepstow with a horse called *Divine Intervention* currently showing good form, and at 12-1 was worth the risk.

So deep in thought was he, the vicar didn't notice the young man with tripod and video camera perched on one of the older graves casually smoking a hand-rolled cigarette, but as he walked past dreaming of equine glory, the stranger, whose name was Neville Bell - Nev to his friends - took it as his cue that the funeral's kick-off wouldn't be far off and tossed the half-finished cigarette aside and set to work. He was anxious for this job to go well after a few recent mishaps. For the past few months, Nev had moved away from videoing weddings and into the more artistic and sombre genre of funerals.

No more for him the long days of shooting grinning bridesmaids and nervous brides, and countless montage edits of drunk couples smooching to Robbie Williams or Chris de Burgh for he had seen a hole in the market.

Infact, he had seen a whole new market in which his Art would be stretched. He had visions of himself as the Bergman of the funeral video genre. He would film in black and white; indulge himself in the long take, the sweeping track and pan, the sensitive close-ups of veil-shrouded widows crushed by grief. He would add emotive non-diegetic soundtracks to create truly moving accounts of the final journey of his clients. Word would get around of just how tasteful this new film-maker was in capturing the moment with a well-chosen cutaway at just the right time and the money would roll in.

Except the money hadn't rolled in, and that was probably down to the fact that so far his endeavours at emulating his Scandinavian auteur hero had yet to find a successful funeral in which to showcase his flare for the maudlin.

That was until today.

Like the vicar, Nev had high hopes for the funeral of Harold Hedley Hegley-Stone. Research had suggested that some of the great-and-the-good of Folkestone were connected to him, and as such would doubtless be attending his final public outing. Moreover, they were mostly of an age themselves where Nev could be looking at future clients, and he wanted to impress. He patted the box of business cards in his pocket that he intended to hand out at the end of the service.

To this end he had laboured long over the pre-production. He had visited the church and its grounds as part of his location recce, taken pictures of the interior and exterior and then drawn up detailed storyboards. It was then, and only then, when he had an impressive pre-production portfolio, that he approached Hegley-Stone's family with his suggestion that he record for posterity the sad day; and was thrilled when they agreed. Admittedly he'd laid the deceased's importance to the town on with a trowel, even going as far as likening his funeral to that of Sir Winston Churchill's, but the lather and flannel had paid off and he was given the green light. From that moment on he was convinced that his future as a funeral filmmaker was bright.

Thoughts of cinematic greatness swirled around his head as he went through the process of setting up, and such was his reverie that he was oblivious of the hearse, long and black as it turned silently in off the road and made its creeping way up through the small graveyard towards the church doors.

Having set up the tripod and locked it in place, Nev bent over to unclip the camera case and lift out his new HD camera that formed the lion's share of the investment in his new venture '*Goodbye Films*'. As he did so, the hearse glided silently past as a ghost so that by the time he'd pulled the camera out and straightened up, it had turned at the front of the church and come to a halt by the doors.

The camera took less than a minute to be attached to the tripod base plate and Nev was now ready to take his place behind the camera. Flipping open the side of the camera he saw a totally black screen and smiled to himself. Leaving the lens cover on was a classic, textbook error. With a flick of the switch the cover slid back and the view-screen was filled with a stone angel in extreme close-up.

By the time Nev had altered the focus, the funeral directors and pall bearers had slid the coffin out of the back of the hearse and had lifted it silently onto their shoulders just as Nev panned the camera round to frame the church door. What came up in the viewfinder was not expected.

And neither was his response: "Oh…shit!" he said aloud. Hefting the tripod up on his shoulder he ran across the graves of the long dead towards the hearse. "No!" he called out in what sounded like a loud stage whisper, "Stop! I say…"

But it was too late; the serene procession had begun and was not to be stopped. Neither, for that matter, was Nev who weaved around the pallbearers and stopped at the door, heaving for breath so hard that it would have surprised no one if he were to be the funeral directors' next customer.

"Sorry, but I'm supposed to be capturing Mr. Hegley-Stone's arrival…" he flashed his business card as a plainclothes CID might, "Goodbye Films".

"What are you saying?" asked the funeral director, "that we rewind?"

"Exactly!" he said and set the tripod down by the door just as he spied the cortege of mourners' cars drawing up at the gate, "before the cast turn up!"

Nev smiled, he did so like it when people shared his wavelength it made things so much simpler.

Nev's attempts at remaining anonymous throughout the rest of the service hadn't gone exactly to plan. His various efforts at capturing Harold Hedley Hegley-Stone's final appearance had met with varying degrees of success. Every time he moved his tripod from one set-up to another during the service he received stern, disapproving looks from some of the older mourners who failed to appreciate what he was trying to achieve.

Even the vicar, initially quite enthusiastic about the idea of recording the deceased's final journey, had begun to appear agitated as Nev crouched beneath the pulpit lining up a particularly artistic low angle medium close-up.

By the time the service had ended, and the coffin borne out on the shoulders of the pallbearers towards the graveyard he had been left behind in the church trying to man oeuvre himself and his camera so that he was able to capture the transition to the place of internment.

Sensing that if he didn't assert himself now, he would miss all the photo opportunities the burial clearly offered the true film-maker, he swallowed hard and pushed forward through the gathering mourners.

"Excuse me, sorry. Can I just... Thank you," he said beginning to plough through the mourners and not waiting for a reply, "Excuse me... cameraman coming through. Make way!"

As he marked his progress with the occasional nudge, bustle and trodden toe, the mood of the mourners grew darker and more antagonistic the nearer he got to the graveside.

Eventually he found himself beside a pile of muddied earth that had been dug out to create the grave and decided that it would provide a suitable vantage point above the mourners and the pallbearers from which to capture the vicars final words before the coffin was lowered into its final resting place.

Slowly he dug the tripods legs into the soil and leant on it as he pulled himself up and then attached the camera back onto the plate-head.

The faces, already stern from mourning, took on malevolent sneers as they realized the camera was panning across, past them to rest on the coffin. For the first time today, however, Nev felt that he had nailed the money shot as he held onto the tripod arm and waited for the vicar to end his graveside eulogy and gesture to the pallbearers to loosen the straps under the coffin.

"That's lovely," he muttered to himself as the camera came to rest on the wreath sitting atop the casket. "Keep her steady... No looking at the camera. That's it. Oh yes. Lovely."

Such was his enthusiasm at finally having secured himself a position that not only gave him an unfettered view of the proceedings but also kept him at arms length from the most vociferous mourners, that he didn't notice his elevation begin to drop. Ever so slightly at first his descent into the pile of mud was imperceptible, but as he gathered momentum, and the heads of the mourners all began to rise up into the shot, blocking the coffin, Nev realised he was sinking and had to remedy it.

One of his shoes came off partially as he pulled himself out of the mud, holding onto the camera that was still filming. But there was no time to waste on erecting the tripod again. The coffin was about to be lowered into the grave. And he was now stuck behind some rather sturdy looking mourners.

Taking hold of the tripod by its legs he began to try and push his way through with varying degrees of success.

"Excuse me...can you just..." he said, easing his way in between the bodies. Some of the women were crying into their handkerchiefs at the sight of Harold Hedley Hegley-Stone disappearing into the round. Grown men either bowed their heads in reflection or stared straight ahead, stone faced as they thought of the man they once knew, how he would have relished the gravitas of the service and the kind words that all who had spoken had uttered. In amongst all the collected sadness and grief came an irritant, nudging, pushing, urging himself forward with his blessed camera.

"Sorry about this...quickly, quickly," he said as he reached two mourners who were not moving aside. By the time a hissed "Shift!" caused them to part, Nev's heart which had lifted at the sight of the graveside suddenly fell as he realised he had just missed the most important shot of the entire shoot.

The coffin was in the grave.

Now was not the time for niceties and funeral etiquette. He had promised the family a production which successfully encapsulated the old mans' final journey, and there was no two ways around it.

He needed that last shot.

Breathing deeply he adopted the best directorial voice he could muster, raised himself up to his full height and said, "Umm... that's great, but do you think we could just do that last shot again? Mmm? Once more, with feeling!"

3

To Rock it seemed like his relationship with Sally has always been like a fully inflated balloon. They had had bobbed and floated through their life together; bouncing lightly off shared experiences, rebounding slowly as away from problems unaffected by what they used to call 'the grown-up world'.

It had always been 'us against the rest'. They had kept each other warm in the glow of their love for each other, deaf to the comments of their unsuitability for each other that came in the form of friendly advice from those who thought they knew best.

Sally kept him grounded. He kept her young. Together they were carefree and invincible. But recently that balloon had begun to sag. Imperceptible sad creases had appeared and the grown-up world had started to weigh heavy around them.

Familiarity, which had once provided the glue that kept them together, had now begun to sprout, if not contempt, at best the green shoots of disaffection. The differences, once embraced, now a wedge.

Sally had started making noises that sounded to him like conformity; applying for jobs that yelled long-term career prospects and holding up a mirror to their lives that saw them both in suits and unhappy.

Rock had done what he'd always done when responsibility came knocking. He pretended it wasn't happening in the hope that it would go away and leave them alone.

A head in the sand always worked wonders. Only this time it did not. The longer he ignored the problem the worse it became. The cancer had set in. With every new job application rejection Sally, who once shone with fun and optimism, began to dim. Now every time he thought of her he saw not iridescence and light, but grey. And with every darkening shade, the balloon sagged a bit further, but still they bobbed about together both ignoring the air that was seeping quietly out of their relationship.

And while Sally busied herself with the distraction of application form after application form, and tweaked and updated her CV to fit each and every new vacancy that arose, Rock chose jobs that offered fun. Short term summer jobs, selling ice cream, working the slot machines in the amusement arcades. And if the job came with a wacky costume - such as an in store demonstrator of clothes protector spray dressed as a moth - all the better.

If pressed, he would say that the fortnight spent dressed as '*Pat the Pasty*', wandering the local supermarket with trays full of mini Cornish pasties, was infinitely more fun than the six months spent in a call centre making outbound calls selling pet insurance. Infact the only redeeming feature of the call centre job was meeting Lexxie, a bubbly red-headed hippy who had arrived in his last week and made up for the previous dreary months with her crazy, upbeat take on life.

It was Lexxie with her eye on the screwball and the kooky, who had spotted the advert for the latest position of *'funployment'* and persuaded Rock to apply which led to them handing out leaflets to the newly opened attraction: *Shepway Life of the Sea* dressed as seagulls. Luckily the costume meant that the hood that served as the gulls head, and the strap on beak at least served as a suitable disguise, so the ignominy of waddling through the pedestrianized town centre as a giant sea-bird was at least masked.

The shoulder bag that contained the flyers didn't seem to be getting any emptier as time went on. This was mainly down to the fact that whenever a passer-by spotted a man-sized seagulls waddling uncomfortably towards them with an outstretched wing waving a piece of A5, they invariably moved quickly in the opposite direction.

But at least the lunch hour was over, which meant those office workers who had come out for sandwiches and a quick pint were now safely back at work, taking their vocal ridicule with them. Now all that was left were pensioners out for a totter or some dejected *'Stay-cationers'* wandering aimlessly around the town with their children whose little faces lit up on sight of a six-foot seagull on a paper round.

"How long have we got to keep this up?" asked Rock as yet another passer-by suddenly ducked into a bric-a-brac shop rather than accept a proffered flyer off a seabird.

"We're here 'til five," Lexxie replied with a comical flap of her wings. Rock smiled. It was typical of her that she could offset the gloom of such a flat and undemanding job with a smile and a joke and make it that all-important word: FUN.

"Come on," she said, "let's head down to the harbour."

As she was about to turn right, Rock sensed something out of the corner of his eye coming towards them at speed and grabbed her arm, pulling her towards him in time to avoid being mowed down by the convoy of three mobility scooters that hurtled past them with no care for the pedestrians who leapt out of their crazed path.

Lexxie looked up at his face and the beak that had swung round in the sudden movement. "My hero!" she said breathlessly. This time they both laughed.

*

Horry had long ago foregone the trappings of house and garden and job. It was also possible that he had foregone the trappings of a marriage too, but it was so long ago, in another lifetime, that he couldn't be sure whether he'd ever been married or not. Certainly his current itinerant lifestyle didn't suggest he could ever have been the marrying kind.

After years of traveling the highways and byways of South East England he had washed up on the pebbly shores of Folkestone and stayed.

He would sometimes stray through Sandgate to Hythe and even sometimes be seen on the road West towards Dymchurch; be spotted in and around Cheriton to the North or even, on the odd occasion, was known to have ventured up onto the cliffs by Capel-le-Ferne bound for Dover but for the majority of the time he was a fixture in Folkestone, just like the William Harvey statue which stood looking out across the English Channel with right hand on heart, left hand holding one and a seagull more than often perched unceremoniously on his head. The only difference between the two - medical discovery and death apart - was that townsfolk and tourists actually took more notice of Horry than the physician who detailed the circulation of blood round the body via the heart.

This afternoon, sensing it was probably the tail-end of lunchtime given the amount of unfinished pints of beer he'd managed to mine sweep in the last half-an-hour, he was picking his way through a litter bin in search of some foodstuff to soak up his liquid intake. He didn't want to totter through town giving the impression that he was no more than a drunken old tramp. If he had one thing, it was pride.

"Eureka!" he announced triumphantly as his fingers curled round a partially eaten M&S sandwich still in its plastic container. He pulled it from the bin like a trawler-man hauling in his latest catch and licked his lips expectantly.

"Awright, Horry?" asked Nev as he trudged past with his camera bag over his shoulder and a twisted tripod under one arm. His trousers were muddied and he looked thoroughly depressed with himself. The experience at the graveside had dampened his mood; not to mention the verbal assault he'd suffered at the hands of...well, pretty much everyone at the funeral or so it seemed to him as he'd been hauled away from the grave by his lapels, and ejected unceremoniously from the graveyard with he considered unnecessary force.

"Crab!" smiled Horry smiled, having taken a bite of the sandwich after a judicious sniff.

Nev looked at Horry tucking into his dubiously acquired provender and wondered whether the quality of his own days would one day be measured by the chance findings in the town's bins. If today's fiasco was anything to go by, he wouldn't bet against it. Shrugging his bag a little higher onto his shoulder he moved on. It was no use sharing his woes with Horry, because whenever he had in the past he'd always managed to come off feeling even worse which to him shouldn't have been right.

Stepping off the curb he was almost run down by three mobility scooters carrying three lively

OAPs. The scourge of Folkestone.

"Oi!" complained Nev, "don't you have horns?" and to his dismay was flicked the bird by the third elderly buggie as it whistled past.

"Did you see that?" he asked. But Horry was already moving away in the opposite direction, no doubt in search of a discarded dessert.

4

In a lay-by on the clifftops in the shadow the Martello Tower, one of the circular defences built during the Napoleonic War to guard against attack from the French that were scattered along this part of the south coast, business at the burger van had not picked up all day. Customer after customer, if they hadn't complained hadn't exactly performed cartwheels at the sight of their burger either.

Gradually Gasmark's mood had become more and more despondent until right now, as he looked at the burger he was about to serve the customer, he could take it no longer. As he opened the bap and automatically reached for the excuse for lettuce he looked at the burger.

The customer, clearly expecting something more mouth watering, also looked at the burger. And together, for this fleeting moment, they were joined. Slowly their disappointed eyes met and Gasmark knew what he had to do. He picked up the limp sliver of meat and spun it out towards the waiting gulls where it flew like a wet cloth Frisbee before landing with an apologetic 'slap' on the grass.

Gasmark opened the till, retrieved the customers' money and handed it back to him. "I'm sorry," he said. And then, with a sudden pang of guilt, pulled a can of Coke from under the counter and handed it across. "Here, have this."

"Ta," the customer said and with a click and hiss of an opened can, walked back to his car. Letting out a long and defeated sigh, Gasmark turned towards Sally who was sitting on the steps of the burger van, idly flicking through a recipe book that she'd picked up in a second-hand bookshop on the way to work that morning.

"Another unsatisfied customer," he said. Without looking up she said, "That's the third today."

"Don't I know it," Gasmark said, sitting beside her.

For a moment they were silent. He looking out over the Channel, eyes full of regret, and she flicking through the last few pages of the book that had reached the desserts section. Closing its covers and bringing it up to her chest to hug it, she turned and said unexpectedly: "I've been thinking...you need to branch out. Give dodgy burgers the boot."

"In favour of what?" he asked, quite ready to shoot down a fresh idea before it could find its wings, " This is a burger van, Sal."

Sally got to her feet and hopped off the step onto the ground where she turned with the elegance of an understudy dancer who had waited too long for the lead to fall ill, and had lost some of the grace of a natural ballerina.

"That's where you're wrong. It's a van..." she paused, raising a finger before making what she thought was her killer point, "that just *happens* to sell burgers."

"...or not as the case may be", Gasmark replied, pouring yet more water on the topic.

But Sally had been thinking this through over the last few weeks as she witnessed satisfaction in the burger vans' customer base all but flat line, and wasn't going to be deterred.

"What you need is a revamp. A makeover!" She threw her arms out and spun on her toes. Gasmark thought fleetingly of Julie Andrews. He rested back on his elbows as she continued.

"Rebranding is all the thing," she said practically brimming with excitement, "Reinvent yourself!"

"As what?" he asked almost automatically, his attention suddenly distracted by a Jaguar XJS that had pulled in off the road and was now making its bumpy way slowly across to where the van was sparked.

"...the Invisible Man?" he asked as the Jaguar pulled up.

A look of concern washed across his face as the driver's door opened and a tall balding mountain of a man stepped out, stood for a moment adjusting his jacket and then, after two equally stocky but not quite as tall gorillas climbed out of the rear doors, began to approach the van.

"A minute o' yer time, Gobshite," the balding mountain said over the wind. His Glaswegian accent anachronous this far south.

"The name's Gasmark," he corrected as the businessman everyone knew simply as Lenny took a record book out from his inside pocket and flicked through to the page he was looking for.

"Whatever," he said, ignoring Gasmark's correction, "Now, what is it you owe today?"

"There's a bit of a problem, Lenny. Things are a little slow just now," Gasmark explained.

"I don't give a monkey's what speed things are, chef boy. Ya ken the score, pay up or drop out," Lenny said and then simply nodded to the two gorillas. "Give him some thinking time." Without saying a word they approached, took him firmly by each arm and lifted him towards the edge of the cliff.

Moments later he was hanging upside down over the edge of the cliff all too aware that a word from their boss and Scotty and Bill would simply let go and allow gravity do the rest. He tried to focus on what Lenny was saying. Clearly saying the right thing in reply was the difference between a safe return to the top of the cliff and being scraped up off the cliff floor and deposited in a Dolmio jar.

To his horror he saw Lenny turn and walk away from the cliff as he yelled up, "But I haven't got it!"

Back at the van events had moved so quickly that Sally hadn't even been able to put up a spirited struggle to stop the two thugs manhandling Gasmark towards the edge of the cliff. Now, seeing Lenny turn and walk back towards her, she feared the worst.

"You've got no right..." she began as Lenny came within talking distance.

"He owes me..."

"Yeah, and if you drop him off a cliff you'll never get your money back."

Lenny moved close towards Sally, causing her to back away but found the path blocked by the van itself. She looked up as the tall silhouette loomed over her...and smiled. "That's business, doll," he said, "Whereas you an' me... that could be nothing but pleasure."

He allowed this suggestion to hang repulsively in the air for a second or two, before he moved past Sally and stepped into the van.

The till, once opened, didn't seem to impress him either, but he took out the brace of five-pound notes and placed them in his wallet before wiping his hands with the tea towel that was sitting on the counter.

"But I take your point...and besides, I'm not totally wi'out remorse." Lifting his right hand to his mouth he whistled across to Scotty who turned to see his boss motion with his thumb to bring Gasmark back up.

"Never let it be said that I'm no' fair." Sally breathed an audible sigh of relief as Gasmark, now set the right way up, walked back towards the van, still shaken and red faced.

"You live to fry another day," Lenny said. "I'm givin' you a month to get your act together, or next time the flying lessons come free. Understood?"

"Understood," Gasmark said, catching the tea towel that Lenny tossed at him.

"Good," he said, before returning his attention to Sally, "If I were you, darlin', I'd start lookin' for another job," before walking back to his car. Scotty and Bill, straightening their jackets as best they could with their outsize frames followed after.

"I need a drink," was all he could say.

5

There was laughter and general bar-room joie de vivre in the pub overlooking the harbour, but none of it was coming from the table in the corner. Gasmark sat cradling a pint. Nev had met up with his flatmate at the van and after the day he'd had, decided that a maudlin evening was probably as good as the day was going to end; and Sally didn't feel like going back to her flat to spend another evening arguing with Rock. So they sat like depressed outcasts on the fringes of the revelry.

"What am I gonna do? I can't even afford to pay *you* properly," Gasmark said looking up woefully at Sally from his pint.

"When's the next ferry to Calais?" asked Nev trying to raise spirits with what he regarded as gallows humour.

"Funny man," said Sally emptily.

"At least it would get me across the Channel. That was always the intention when I first arrived here. Have I told you about the mugging?" Gasmark asked.

"Yes," Sally and Nev chorused. It was an all-too-familiar story.

"But you never explained what you were going to do once you arrived," Sally added, taking another sip of her drink.

"Isn't it obvious, Sal? I'm a chef. It's my

spiritual home. It's where I belong."

"Can you speak French?" she asked.

"Not exactly."

"Ah. There you go then," she said and they lapsed once more into silence, which was broken finally by Nev who'd decided that enough was enough and there must be some sort of light at the end of this gloomy tunnel.

"You two are a bundle of laughs today," he said finishing his pint, "same again?"

Gasmark drained what was remaining in his glass and handed it up to Nev who was already on his feet. "Cheers. Sal...?"

Sally covered her glass with her hand, "I'm fine thanks, Nev."

As Nev made for the bar across the reasonably crowded room, Sally looked at Gasmark and her heart went out to him. He was so full of dreams, but lacked the final push to make them a reality. Infact not a million miles away from Rock with whom he shared similar qualities. Qualities she'd found attractive once upon a time, but now had recently begun to find increasingly irritating and oppressive.

But not in Gasmark.

She reached across and touched his knee.

"You okay? Really?" she asked softly.

Gasmark looked up at her and found that he was looking directly into her deep brown eyes and for a moment, something stirred and he found himself adrift. But just as quickly so as not to make the moment awkward, he pulled himself back. "I'm fine. Y'know, having been hung over a cliff and threatened with the same next month, but without the safety net. Yeah, never better. Where am I going to find the money? Another loan?"

It was the first loan off Lenny that had got him into this situation in the first place. The Scotsman had seen in a desperate Gasmark the opportunity to not only shift the burger van and all his backlog of stock, but also to tie it into a suffocating loan that he was guaranteed never to pay back whilst at the same time making it look like a fortuitous and supportive business partnership.

The realization that it was anything but came too late for him to back out of the arrangement and now he was stuck with a business that was going nowhere and any profits that were made went straight back to Lenny by way of overdue interest.

"It's like I said..." Sally was explaining, "you need to branch out."

"How? People don't want fancy food from a burger van."

"Then we're just going to have think of some gimmick that'll change their minds." There seemed to him that there was fire in those eyes, but he looked away too soon to be sure. His life was complicated enough at the moment without adding another layer to it.

At the bar, Nev was trying his best to get the attention of the barman to no avail. In a desperate measure he slapped a £10 note on his forehead.

"Shop!" But it didn't work. Partly because he'd chosen the exact same moment as the entry to the pub by two seagulls which caused all eyes to look away from the bar.

Gasmark too tried to change the subject away from his own woes. "Where's Rock tonight?"

"Who knows?" she shrugged, "who cares?"

"What's up with you two lately?"

"I dunno," Sally admitted with an imperceptible sigh, "we used to have fun and laugh and do all that together stuff, but now everything he does annoys me. All these jobs he gets and then jacks in. It's no way to carry on, is it?"

"If it's so bad why don't you call it a day?" It was a clumsy remark and as soon as he'd said it he wished he hadn't, but Sally didn't register.

"Sometimes it's just easier to stay put."

"Hello..." Gasmark said in an attempt to move the conversation away from the potential choppy waters into which he had inadvertently navigated, "...looks like Nev's pulled a bird."

Sally followed Gasmark's eye line. At that moment Nev was involved in what looked like a flirtatious conversation with a giant female seagull who was trying her best to get him to accept a leaflet that he was unable to take, owing to the two pint glasses in his hand. Instead, he took it between his teeth and headed back towards them.

Such was their distraction with Nev and his seagull, that neither Gasmark nor Sally noticed Rock, still in his seagull costume, approaching them.

"Shepway Life of Sea?" he asked, holding out a flyer.

"No thanks… keep it," Sally said dismissively before looking up, "Oh…my…God," she said, finding herself looking straight into the face of her boyfriend, "You have *got* to be joking."

Rock was oblivious to the fact that he looked ridiculous, and in order to get the full effect, he held his wings out wide: "What do you think?"

"This'd be a new job then would it, Rock?" said Gasmark taking a flyer and reading. "*The Shepway Life of Sea*. What's this?"

"Ten per cent off if you turn up with the voucher."

Sally was still reeling with the reality of the situation. This was as far from the job in advertising Rock had told her about was likely to get. "You're handing out leaflets?"

"Incognito… so it won't affect my long term career."

"What career?" she said, her voice rising, "
Your idea of a long-term job is if you go back the second week! Jesus, Rock!" and before the tears could spill from her eyes, she got to her feet and made her way clumsily out the pub just as Nev arrived back at the table with two pints and the girl in a seagull costume.

"They didn't have pork scratchings, so I went

for the seabird alternative!"

"I better go after her," Rock said and followed in Sally's wake.

Nev handed Gasmark a pint, "Was it something I said?"

"More like something Rock said," replied Gasmark taking the glass, "or rather had not said."

6

The air in the office of the Environmental Health department this particular lunchtime was heavy. The air conditioning was broken and no one had been able to locate the set of keys that opened the windows.

A small fan sat on a vacant desk and did its best to circulate the static air, but every wheeze of its rotation only served to confirm that it was punching well above its weight and failing. What the office needed was a bigger, more robust fan, with multiple speeds and used to dealing with the circulation of great roomfuls of air.

The very occasional and tired wafts from one side of the room to the other appeared as languid as the mood that had led to the Environmental Health Officers deciding on a two-hour lunch break, so at least now there was less heat being generated by the bodies at their workstations.

All except one.

While everybody else had jumped at the opportunity to spend two hours away from the office in the nearest pub, Leonard Fowler had not. He sat at his desk, the remains of a packed lunch rolled up in a piece of aluminum foil, writing up his latest follow-up report on the newly opened Kebab shop on the outskirts of town.

He had been more than satisfied upon his return to see that his recommendations to replace the rucked linoleum floor had been acted upon. The whole place had been repainted and every surface cleaned so that it fairly sparkled in the summer sun that dared to intrude the virtually now sterile environment.

What he had failed to realize, and would have done had he proofread his original report, was that his recommendation, due to a typing error, had actually stated the '*Lino flooring was fucked*'. However, the message that came across was that Fowler was not a Health Inspector to be messed with, and the owner of the Kebab shop had moved quickly to get the floor replaced and the whole area redecorated. Whatever the cause, Fowler had been impressed, and given the premises a clean bill of health.

The clocked on the wall dragged itself to announce the second hour of the afternoon with two consumptive electronic chimes. Fowler instinctively checked his wristwatch to find, yet again, that Council Time had dropped five minutes.

He was an odd looking man. A nose that seemed slightly too big for his face and eyes that were definitely too small giving the appearance of a rat looking into the convex side of a spoon for its missing whiskers. His hair, parted at the side, was lank and wispy in places. In strong wind one could definitely see bald patches in progress, but normally he appeared as hirsute as a man approaching late middle age had any reason to expect. He was precise about his appearance yet not fussy, but there was something about him that singled him out from the rest of the younger Environmental Health Officers, especially Ashley, the loud, boorish man who sat opposite him. He lacked a sense of humour and as such might as well have had a hand-painted target on his back and a sign around his neck that read: 'Victim'.

There was a sudden noise further down the corridor that marked the return of his colleagues from their liquid lunch. Fowler sighed at the prospect of the office being filled with seven slightly drunk Health Inspectors all adding their beer-breath and tobacco aroma to the already stale atmosphere, and was glad that he'd booked in a visit to a Fijian restaurant in Hythe which would take him most of the afternoon. But first there was the return to endure and it began, as it always did, with Ashley bursting through the door.

"Hey Fowler...take a look at this!" he announced standing framed in he doorway brandishing what appeared to be an outsize spud gun, "The latest in tranquillizer guns for the pest control guys. Guaranteed to take out vermin at twenty paces."

He lifted it, aimed at what he imagined was a cornered vermin and squinted as if peering through a telescopic lens. "You dirty rat!" and pretended to shoot, "Kapow! What d'ya think?" he asked, pausing to blow imaginary smoke from the end of the barrel like the seasoned Western gunslinger he wasn't.

For his part Fowler stood up and filled his briefcase with the files that he had been working on for the past two hours. "I haven't got time for toys, Ashley, when there are restaurants out there breaking God-knows-what hygiene rules."

"And'll still be breaking them in half an hour...lighten up."

But Fowler was not to be mollified, "You know how fast bacteria multiplies. In thirty minutes we could be looking at an epidemic!"

"In this town?" he laughed.

Fowler brushed past him, "Excuse me, but I have lives to save."

The remaining group of Health Inspectors who'd been enjoying the exchange blocked his path to the coat rack. Irritably Fowler cut through them until he was able to grab at his jacket, and then pushed through the door and into the corridor where he breathed out, ready for the wave of hysterics he was sure would come. And after they had chorused: "Ooh...get her!" the laughter broke upon the shores as he knew it surely would.

Shrugging his jacket on, he put a dignified distance between himself and the unprofessional drunken rabble he had the misfortune of calling his colleagues. He had important work to do, even if they didn't.

*

The houses that overlooked the seafront bore a majesty that belonged to a long dead and dust covered past. The façades wearily displayed their age through the cracked windows, peeling paint and crumbling masonry at the edges. Tiles slipped, some often fell and smashed during the high winds that whipped the south coast during the off-season winter months, never to be replaced.

The glory days that had seen Edwardian gentlemen stroll arm-in-arm with parasol-twirling ladies had vanished forever. Resurrected only in romanticized paintings and viewed through jerky cine-footage in the local museum. Everyone wore hats, men sported Saxcoberg-popular beards and women clad in all-over body swimsuits dipped tentative toes in the bracing sea.

The houses heaved with life and light and laughter. The well to do of the town threw parties to announce weddings, christenings, birthdays and sundry other anniversaries. The light spilled out onto the seafront so that the lesser classes could see the beauty contained in these lives. The houses, all grand echoed this self-importance. The balconies screamed elegance, the pillared front doors purred wealth and the wide steps leading up to these demi-palaces suggested opulence.

However, that was all in the past. Two world wars and a whole cultural shift away. Now these houses were not occupied by wealthy families - except the end house that still belonged to Mrs. Hart-Silver who still clung to life with the tenacity of someone who had lived through the hard times but still recalled the good no matter how long ago they'd occurred. She steadfastly refused to move out - despite many lucrative offers by mercenary property investors eying her house enviously. The family money, which had been made in preserves and pickles during the height of the Empire had, like a once powerful river, dwindled to a trickle of a stream and now allowed the widow to live out the remainder of her years if not in the manner in which she had for so long been accustomed, at least independent of social care. What it didn't stretch to, of course, was regular maintenance of the building. Like its owner, gently faded, it now stood along with its neighbours looking out on a world of which it was no longer a part.

Property investors and private landlords who lived most of the year abroad in Portugal or Spain or even Croatia owned he rest of these houses. And where, like Mrs. Hart-Silver, there were once families and multiple bedrooms, bathrooms and reception rooms the property developers had carved up the interiors into a myriad of single rooms, studio flats and attic apartments that stolethe soul from the houses and replaced them with students, the unemployed, the low paid, the Benefit class.

In short, these houses offered, for Rock and Lexxie, the best and easiest way to offload many flyers for the *Shepway Life of Sea*. And so too did the cars all parked up along the curb.

Rock was just lifting up a windscreen wiper to plant a flyer on another MPV when he saw the door to Mrs. Hart-Silver's house open and Nev appear on the doorstep. He was about to lift a wing in greeting when he witnessed the formidable old lady come at Nev with a walking stick raised amidst cries of: "It's a disgrace", "...should be ashamed..." and "...the word is ghoulish!" until he had been forced down two of the wide steps before a shoulder bag with portfolios found wings and was thrown out after him. He vaguely heard a rather plummy voice declare: "...the very thought of it," before the door was slammed shut, dislodging some sizable flakes of paint into the bargain.

"Another satisfied customer?" Rock asked as Nev approached rubbing his shoulder where a bruise was sure to arrive, "Who was that, a merry widow?"

"Bloody woman. You'd think at her age she'd be grateful of the attention."

Nev's umbrage was cut short by the caw cawing of a seagull, the sound of squealing brakes and a thud; then just as fast, the squeal of tyres as the Jaguar XJS roared off.

Lenny's Jaguar had hit a seagull and driven away. Lexxie, in her costume dropped her bag of flyers and ran over to where the felled bird lay, flapping its wings in the last panicked spasm of death. It was an altogether peculiar sight as she knelt over the stricken bird.

Nev and Rock - who was also still in his

costume - ran over.

"What happened?"

Lexxie looked up, tears in her eyes and pointed after the departing car, "That idiot in the car ran straight into it. Didn't even stop."

"But you're okay?" Nev asked.

Lexxie nodded, and wiped a tear from her cheek with her left wing. "I'm fine, but this chap..."

Rock bent to pick up the bird that had now stopped moving. As he lifted it the head lolled to one side.

"Is it definitely *dead*?" asked Nev.

"Looks like it, but if you'd like a second opinion...here," he replied handing it over before turning his attention to Lexxie. "What you need is a stiff drink."

Rock pulled the larger of the two seagulls up off the pavement as Nev held the dead bird out at arms length. Holding a still warm corpse of one made him more than a little uneasy. Its warmth and surprisingly heavy weight gave the impression that it might suddenly return to life with a jerk, and the thought of such a resurrection made him shiver.

"What d'you want me to do with this?" he asked.

Rock regarded Nev and his bird, "You always reckon you're the ideas man," he said and walked, with a protective wing around Lexxie's feathered shoulders, off towards the nearest pub, leaving Nev holding the dead seagull.

7

The morning had proved no more productive for Gasmark and Sally. What few customers who had come to the serving hatch had taken one look at the burgers and only bought cans of Cola so that by early afternoon, with no sign of scraps or leftovers, the birds had flown off to pastures new.

"At least we're uncontaminated by food,"

Gasmark had joked thinly in-between sales. Sally looked up from one of the books she'd picked out from the Cookery section of the library. She had brought "*MEAT THE ALTERNATIVES - An introduction to different dishes*" with her in the hope of raising Gasmark's spirits.

"How about cooking Ostrich?" she suggested. Gasmark shrugged, "Too tough."

"Kangaroo then?"

"Too chewy."

Sally ran her finger down the list, "Giraffe... Zebra... Ooh, here's a good one... Alligator!"

For the first time in days Gasmark's mouth broadened into a sort of smile, "An alligator? In Folkestone?"

Sally acknowledged the suggestion as amusing, "Not alligators then?"

"No."

It was at this point as they ran through a list of

possible alternatives to beef or chicken that the unexpected happened. A dead seagull was slapped down onto the counter.

Having been left holding the dead gull in the street by Lexxie and Rock, Nev had been keen to get rid of it as soon as possible, but as he stood over the litterbin about to drop it in he noticed a polystyrene takeaway container and a half-eaten burger and had had a brainwave.

Instead of disposing of it there, he had swung the dead bird over his shoulder and turned towards the cliff top that overlooked the town with an unorthodox suggestion very much in mind.

And so it was that he arrived at the van at precisely the apposite moment in the conversation about alternative foodstuffs with his own suggestion:

"How about seagull?"

"An interesting opening gambit," said Gasmark, "what's wrong with '*Hello*'?"

Sally didn't look up from the book, but instead was flicking through the pages, "I don't think it mentions seagulls..." before looking up straight into the lifeless eye of the bird, and letting out an involuntary shriek.

Gasmark was more balanced. "Nev, what are you doing with a dead seagull?"

"I found it. Now, you're always telling me I don't take enough interest in food, right? Well I watched this programme on some cable channel the other afternoon about alternative foodstuffs...you know, what you can and what you can't eat? So, when this got run over it set me thinking...who's gonna miss a few seagulls? It's not as if they're an endangered species. Least not round here!"

Gasmark rolled the idea round his head before deciding to make sure he'd not misunderstood Nev's suggestion.

"You want me to *cook* seagulls?"

"Yeah, why not?"

"Cos' they'd probably poison you, that's why not." Sally joined in, "And God knows what you'd catch."

But short-term exposure to the television had prepared Nev for the argument, "That's where you're wrong. The bloke on TV reckoned seagulls don't spread food poisoning organisms to humans."

"Really?"
Nev shrugged, "So he said."

Gasmark considered the possibility. He tried to recall whether anything had been said in Catering College about cooking seabirds, but came up blank. However, Sally was thinking ahead.

"If Nev's right, it would be a great gimmick, wouldn't it?"

Gasmark wasn't convinced, "Oh yeah, I can see the headlines now: Local Chef Jailed for Poisoning Customers with Seagulls."

"What have you got to lose?" Nev asked.

"You want a list?"

Sally slammed the cookbook shut with force.

"Come on Gasmark, let's give it a try," and looked first at Gasmark, then at Nev and back to Gasmark. Then they both looked straight at Gasmark giving him the impression that he was being backed into a culinary corner.

*

In the end it wasn't just Gasmark who was responsible for preparing and cooking the dead bird, it was all three of them despite Nev's protestations that he was just not cut out for the job.

Gasmark had assuaged his unease by involving them all; that way if he failed they all failed and he'd feel better about it.

So while he plucked the bird, Sally - ably assisted by Nev despite claiming that he was disable assisting - proceeded to make the batter that Gasmark had decided was perhaps the best way to present this new and undiscovered delicacy.

To his credit, once he'd thought it through and decided that it should at least be attempted, Gasmark had set his mind to the challenge markedly well. He'd reasoned with himself that people ate all sorts of things that the British quaintly considered 'off menu': Badgers, horses, kangaroo testicles, so why not seagulls? At worst they'd be instantly inedible and ripe for spitting out, at best they'd taste like chicken and...well... he figured they'd cross that particular bridge of ethics when (and if) they came to it. As it was, this gastronomic experiment could just be a dish too far; the limb onto which not even Heston Blumenthal would venture out on.

Once the bird had been plucked and washed and the innards removed - a job that had made Nev retch - especially when Gasmark had handed them to him to dispose of - his nimble fingers played over the bird, now indistinguishable as a seagull, jointing it, cutting through the flesh with ease as he divided it up into portions ready for cooking. Both Nev and Sally watched, impressed, as the bird was segmented and divided up - wings, breast, thigh.

At a nod, Sally brought out the bowl of batter and placed it on the counter.

"Ready?" he asked them both. Sally nodded and Nev, himself coated in so much flour that he resembled a ghost, gave an expectant thumbs up.

"Here we go then," he said beginning the process of coating the fillets each with a flamboyant dip in and out of the mixture Sally had whisked up. And then, after they had been coated he placed them into the sizzling fat where they fizzed and sparkled and jumped.

The faces of his two friends were as those of expectant parents awaiting the birth of their first child. Gasmark checked his watch, held the latticed scoop in his other hand and counted down: "Four...three...two...one...stop cooking!" and with the grace of a natural showman scooped the battered fillets and wings and legs out of the fat and onto some kitchen roll where he patted off the excess fat before transferring them to waiting paper plates.

"Et voila!" he announced. For a moment the selection of battered gull sat bathed in a golden glow as the intense heat of the oil reduced and steam rose and curled in an almost sensual dance.

As one all three friends leaned in.

"Well," asked Gasmark, "what are you waiting for? Tuck in!"

Nev looked across to Sally, "Ladies first. Sal..." But Sally demurred, "Er, I'm not actually that hungry just now. You eat it," and pushed the plate towards Nev.

"I can't," he said, pushing it back.

"Why not?"

"I'm a vegetarian. Don't eat meat."

"Since when?" Gasmark asked. As his flatmate, this was news to him.

Nev shrugged nonchalantly, hoping that he wasn't called to explain himself further,

"Recently."

It was clear what was happening. The sudden rush of idea was one thing, but somehow now they were faced with the steaming reality of a cooked seagull, the bravado of the experiment had dissolved like the steam currently dancing its way into the air.

"C'mon guys," said Gasmark more out of desperation than anything else, "someone's gotta eat it."

Sally looked further afield out from the van. The corners of her mouth began forming a smile. The other two followed her gaze.

Horry was having no luck in the bins this morning. So far he had gone through at least twelve, and all he'd found was a squashed and fly-covered Mars bar which he'd passed on. As a rule he never ate chocolate, as it was bad for his teeth. Now, as lunch approached, his hunger increased. He'd scoured the trail of litterbins up onto the cliff top that overlooked the harbour side of the town and was currently rummaging deep into the one next to the Martello tower but wasn't having any more luck than his previous attempts elsewhere in the town.

Just then he caught something on the breeze; a sweet succulent aroma that immediately made his mouth water. He stopped searching for a moment and just enjoyed the smell that seemed to be coming from the van by the lay-by.

He looked towards it, and noticed that the nice girl who always said hello to him as she cycled past of a morning was walking towardshim like an apparition. He shook his head and blinked. The pleasant aroma of fried food had affected him in the same way as an oasis affected those lost and thirsty in a desert. Clearly the lack of food was making him hallucinate. Could it be that she was wearing an apron, and carrying a plate piled with food?

Behind her there seemed to be two others carrying cutlery wrapped in a serviette and a large bottle of lemonade.

He shook his head again and blinked, but when he looked once more he found that the apparition was nearly upon him, and the smell, that gorgeous, sumptuous smell of fried batter was wrapping its arms around him in an all consuming caress and drawing him away from the litterbin. Its tendrils carrying him to the picnic table to where Sally had placed the plate of food.

He felt his jaw slacken and some saliva dribble out. He wiped it away with the back of his hand.

*

Much to Horry's relief, the sight of Sally carrying a plateful of steaming, freshly fried food accompanied by the waiter and the chef in an almost magisterial processionin his hour of need was very real indeed.

Having placed the plate down on the table, Sally had asked him whether he was hungry and would he like some food that Gasmark had recently prepared. He had nodded, speech at this point seeming irrelevant, and also difficult due to the possibility of more saliva flooding out of his mouth in expectation of the flavours that - by the smell of it -were just queuing up in the food ready to be released. At which point Nev had whipped out a paper table cloth, Gasmark laid the table andNev had stepped back in to pour some busy looking lemonade into a Styrofoam cup.

"Your table is ready for you now," Sally had announced and, with a bow of the head, Horry had taken his seat place at the table as the three looked on.

"Smells good," he had said, picking up his knife and form and unwrapping them from the serviette.

"Freshly caught and cooked," Gasmark explained, when what he actually meant was freshly knocked down and cooked.

With a flourish, Horry tucked the serviette into his frayed shirt collar and once again picked up the cutlery and began to cut into the first portion.

As one, Gasmark, Nev and Sally leaned in, breath held. Horry brought the first forkful up to his mouth and popped it in. A slight breeze blew around the cliff top, but no one noticed. All eyes were on the tramp. He chewed. Made an appreciative sound. Chewed some more and swallowed. Almost immediately he cut himself another, slightly larger piece and popped that in his mouth. His chewing became faster, the noises more appreciative and the grease dribbling from his chin glistened in the sun.

Finally after they had watched rapt as he hungrily devoured portion after portion of the seagull, Gasmark could take it no more. "Well?" Sally backed him up, "Yeah Horry, what'sit like?" Horry didn't answer straight away. He reached for the lemonade and drained it in one mouthful that was then followed by a loud belch. "Mmm, good. Seagull."

Gasmark was completely wrong footed. He thought he would have to lie and say it was chicken or duck. What he hadn't expected was for his guinea pig to nail the new foodstuff on its first outing. "What makes you say that?" Horry's logic was simple, born perhaps from too many years on he road and one too many meals of dubious origin. "Because, it tastes like seagull."

Nev lifted the Styrofoam cup he'd been holding to his mouth and in his best Texan accent announced triumphantly: "Houston, we have a foodstuff. The seagull has landed!"

*

Nev was busying himself with the rolling of a cigarette, sitting on the side steps of the van while Sally and Gasmark cleaned up and wound down the shutter.

After the success of the seagull experiment earlier that afternoon, Horry had been given a doggy bag and a couple of complimentary cans of drink before he'd said his thanks and goodbyes and wandered off back towards the town in search of some good broadsheet newspapers for something to read later in bed.

Sally had watched him go. A lonely figure, his solitary lifestyle didn't seem to bother him, yet she always felt sad for him. Transference Rock called it during one of their arguments, upon which she'd thrown a cushion at him and shut herself in the bathroom. There was something about Horry that brought about the maternal spirit in her, and the more often she saw him the stronger the desire became to do something to improve his life. Eventually he dipped down out of view and she was left looking at the English Channel.

There was a thin haze over the water giving it a slightly grey blurred impression. Like a matte painting stretched across a soundstage. It all helped to create an otherworldliness about the day that hadn't been what one would generously call 'usual' in any sense of the word ever since Nev had turned up with his road kill and asked Gasmark to cook it.

"Of course, you know what this means in business terms?" asked Nev, having completed his cigarette and now lighting it, "With no capital outlay for product, we're looking at a straight down the line one hundred per cent profit margin!"

Both Gasmark and Sally looked at each other,

"We?" they said together.

"Naturally," explained Nev, "Seeing as it was my idea in the first place! Now all we have to do is catch some more gulls."

"How?" asked Gasmark, already accepting that Nev had appointed himself as co-partner in this possible enterprise.

"I dunno. How hard can it be?"

8

The night blanketed everything in a closeness that foretold a possible thunderstorm. The air seemed dense and coated everything in a heavy, oppressive layer. Windows were kept open, as inhabitants welcomed in whatever breath of a breeze could be tempted across the sil. And those still out felt sluggish and slow.

The sky was black and the dense clouds that moved silently overhead were as limousines cruising the heavens.

The town's seagull population was thinning out as it prepared to roost for the night. No chips to be scavenged, not discarded packet of crisps to be attacked, no tip of saveloy tossed into the gutter to be retrieved and gulped down greedily.

The whole town was sleeping and so were its birds.

Down on the raised shingle beach the small boats used by fishermen had been pulled up away from the shoreline and covered with tarpaulin sheets. The gentle hiss of the sea as it retreated back across the shingle sounded a note of disapproval as Gasmark and Nev, dressed in black crouched behind one of the boats looking decidedly furtive.

"Are you sure this is legal?" Gasmark asked in a whisper, concerned that they weren't breaking the law.

"Now you ask!" Nev peered at his flat mate through the gloom, "Just look on it as doing the Council a favour".

"How do you figure that?"

Nev leaned towards Gasmark, keen not to risk being overheard, "They're desperate to control seagull numbers, but can't do it because all the bird lovers won't let 'em, right?"

"Yeah."

"So, *we* do it instead."

"And turn pests into profit?"

Nev was relieved that Gasmark saw the prospect of what they were about to do in the same clear-cut business terms as he did. For him it was as obvious as the noses on their faces.

"Exactly! We could even end up with the Queen's Award for Industry. This is just how McDonalds started...and look at them now. Global!"

Gasmark didn't share his overly simplistic view, "I don't think they actually mixed fast food with pest control, Nev, but I see your point."

"Good. Now are we gonna sit around here gassing all night or are we going to get ourselves some more of these bloody birds?"

*

The doorbell rang twice before Sally had reached it. Someone was in a hurry, and even before she opened it she knew exactly who.

The sight that greeted her, however, was unexpected. Both Nev and Gasmark were splattered with guano and sported a very liberal coating of white feathers. They looked like they'd run into a Western posse and come out of the exchange a punishment short of tarring. But no matter what their appearance, it was the lone result of the evening's endeavours that caused Sally to utter an admonishing: "One? That's all you got?"

"Don't..." said Nev stepping into the flat followed by Gasmark who was carrying the lone seagull under his jacket, "just don't."

Gasmark, however, had his own view of the enterprise that hadn't yielded what had been expected. "They are *impossible* to catch." Suddenly the shape under his jacket began to move.

"And it's still alive!" she pointed out. She had expected them to bring dead birds to her door, not live ones.

"What are you going to do with it? I'm assuming you're not just going to let it die of old age?"

"Have you got any...pills?" asked Nev.

"Why, has it got a headache?"

"*Sleeping* pills. I read it in a book once, you feed sleeping pills to the birds and presto - Seagulls a la snooze."

"Sleeping pills? You want sleeping pills for a seagull?"

The imploring looks from both Nev and Gasmark suggested they did.

"I must be mad," she said and strode off towards the bathroom. "You do know that when a vet says they're going to put an animal to sleep," she shouted from the bathroom where she was rummaging through the cabinet for the blister pack of Temazepam she was sure was there, "they actually mean kill and not sleep?"

"It's just to put it out while we work a way of...erm...execution," Nev explained somewhat awkwardly. If truth were told, he'd sort of expected Gasmark to be a dab hand at wringing birds' necks, and was mildly put out when it transpired that he wasn't.

"The meat I prepare and cook has always been slaughtered before I get it," he'd explained through gritted teeth as yet another bird had slipped free of their grasp and flown off in a flurry of feathers and noise, "I'm not what you'd call 'hands on' when it comes to killing them."

"Now you tell me!"

The next bird they'd managed to get hold of clearly had other ideas, and still able to move its head, showed just what a well-aimed beak could do. Nev had sprung back clutching his hand and Gasmark, in an attempt to stop the creature for making a run for it had leapt at it seconds too late and found his face covered with the nervous after-effects of a scrambled takeoff.

The more birds they chased, the more exhausted they became. The oppressive heat seemed to have increased as the night went on and caused their clothes to stick to their sweat drenched bodies. By the time they managed to get one and keep hold of it without suffering any injury or indignity, they were beyond killing it.

"Let's just take it back to Sally," Gasmark heaved,

"Maybe she'll have an idea."

"Or a cleaver," gasped Nev.

And so they'd arrived on her doorstep.

"How many do you think you'll need?" Sally asked appearing from the bathroom at last holding the Temazepam.

"I don't know, how strong are they?" asked Nev as if facing a dispensing chemist.

"They're for insomnia, how should I know? Look, take two," she advised with a sudden impish grin on her face, "three times a day," and giggled as she split the pack and two capsules dropped into her hand.

"I'm glad you're finding this funny," Nev said accepting the tablets.

"Can we just hurry up?" Gasmark urged as the seagull got a second wind and struggled, "before we have to chase a free bird round the flat." Holding the pills Nev now seemed at a loss with how to go about what needed doing next. "How are we going to get the tablets down?"

"Bread!" said Sally in a sudden moment of clarity and moved past them in the corridor towards the kitchen. "We'll roll them up in little bread pellets and drop them in and massage the throat so it swallows."

Gasmark followed her, keen to divest himself of the heavy bird.

As he did so there came the sound of hammering from the loft. "What's Einstein up to?" he asked.

"When I told him what you were up to he said he said you'd never be able to catch seagulls without expert equipment and then disappeared up there. Been there ever since. Nev, stick your head up, see what he's doing. We'll feed the bird."

It seemed to Rock that Nev and Gasmark lacked his own peculiar talent in the area of gull catching. Gasmark undeniably had a gastronomic flair but neither he or Nev had been properly equipped when they ventured out this evening. The noises coming from the hallway only served to confirm this.

Rock smiled. This was where he came in. He used to joke that he was a complicated man:

"I come in kit form and very hard to assemble." Sally had long since grown tired of the joke she had heard so often, especially as she had come to view Rock as anything but complicated. But at the heart of the oft-repeated gag lie something resembling a truth. If not a kit-formed human being he had at least grown up obsessed with the idea of assembly.

Rock was a tinkerer. He'd always been fascinated in how things had been put together; how things ticked. From his earliest Airfix model of HMS Belfast to his successful rebuilding of a cuckoo clock that had long since lost its chirpy *'cuckoo!'* And now here was his chance to prove that far from being a bit of a loser good for nothing bar handing out promotional leaflets he had something none of them had: the talent for invention. And so he set to work on the problem at hand – namely how to catch a seagull.

His ideas, to begin with, were grandiose and while looking impressive on paper were somewhat impractical. The nearest he got to second stage design was something resembling a lobster-pot that lured the unwitting seagull in. Once in it was unable to retreat back out and was forced forwards towards a rather sticky end with a slicing blade that left it headless. But it was too big and involved a large dollop of luck in getting the naturally suspicious gull to make its way inside the trap.

Discarding these ideas he returned to the drawing board and sketched his way through another dreary afternoon before deciding he needed inspiration and left the flat bound for the nearest hardware store.

It was there as he stood in an aisle looking at a variety of traps for vermin – some humane others not – that he was struck by the simplest and smallest. In an instant he knew what to do.

Picking up the simple, traditional mouse-trap he paid for it and, with a renewed spring in his step, returned to the flat and his loft-space workspace. Not for the first time thanking his lucky stars that their flat had such a room.

Upon moving in they'd discovered the flat had

an unused, but decidedly spacious loft space and Rock had been beside himself. There had been no ladder, and the hatch had been painted over a few times, but once he'd broken the seal and climbed up through the hatch it was as if he'd discovered Narnia. Sally couldn't see what all the fuss had been about, but such was Rock's boyish enthusiasm that she'd been buoyed along with it.

Once he'd installed a retractable ladder he spent every spare moment up there clearing away the cardboard boxes and years worth of cobwebs and laying down boards and throwing round a coat of paint. Then he bypassed some of the electric circuit and ran up some lights before installing some beanbags and declaring the space well and truly open.

Sally had brought home some champagne and officially opened it and that evening, drinking and laughing in their very own hideaway from the world was one of the happiest she'd spent in the flat.

Gradually, however, as they grew apart, Rock used the space as an annex; somewhere he could retreat to; somewhere he could escape.

Once he'd returned from the hardware store Rock quickly made for the loft and now sat at his workbench with the mouse-trap before him. What had struck him about the trap was it simplicity. A wooden base, a trip for bait and a sensitive spring that released a spring bar with such speed and force it broke the mouse's neck in one lightning quick action.

Forgetting all his complicated, cumbersome designs this small tried and tested method of execution was just the ticket. Not only was it fast and efficient it was also highly portable. Once the gull had been caught and dispatched all that was needed was to re-set the spring and the process could begin all over again. Rock smiled to himself. Now all he needed to do was upsize it.

He had heard the doorbell sound moments ago and the murmur of familiar voices below as they moved further into the flat, but was too wrapped up in his invention to drag himself away. Besides, he thought, once Sally told them what he was building, they were sure to find their up anyway. So he stayed where he was and continued putting the finishing touches to his trap.

And sure enough, before long he was aware of someone clambering up the ladder and the familiar, jovial voice of Nev, "Rock?"

"Up here," he said and only had time to turn away from his Heath-Robinson contraption before he saw Nev's head pop up through the hatchway.

"What's with all the banging?"

"I'm problem solving."

"What's the problem?"

"By the sound of it, your entry into the world of small game hunting didn't exactly cover you with glory." Nev regarded his guano-splattered jacket and shrugged.

"Yeah, it didn't go as planned, to put it mildly. It's like the buggers didn't want to be caught."

"Who'd have thought?" said Rock. "What you need is something more practical."

"Such as?"

Rock turned and pulled up the contraption he'd been working on which looked like a giant mousetrap. With what amounted to a proud flourish he added,

"Ta-dah!"

Nev was none the wiser. "Some mouse!" he said, "What is it...exactly?"

"Behold...the Gull-o-tine."

Possessing the name for the device might have made it more identifiable, but he still didn't understand quite what it did and how their problem was solved. So he said so.

For his part Rock went into explanation mode. "It's easy," he said, "seagull sees the bait something like a sardine. Yum yum yum." He applied some pressure on the trip with a wooden ruler and they both jumped as the trap suddenly leapt off the workbench as the spring-loaded bar whipped across in a hundred and eight degree arc splintering the ruler in two. "And bingo! Dead bird."

Nev's jaw dropped and then as the simplicity of the contraption sank in his mouth then pulled itself into the widest smile it could manage and he looked at Rock who by this time had simply folded his arms, content that his work here was done.

"Rock," he said calmly, "You. Bloody. Genius."

Just then there came an almighty crash from the kitchen and Sally screamed. In an instant both Nev and Rock made for the hatch, clambered down the steps into the hallway and immediately had to duck to avoid a low flying seagull.

Their attempt to feed the Tamazepam to the bird by forcibly opening its beak had brought about a fight or flight reaction in the creature. In a sudden spasmodic movement Gasmark had lost his grip. The bird slipped free from beneath his coat and flapped about under the kitchen table making strangulated caw-caw sounds in its terror. Sally had been so shocked by the eruption of what she had up until now considered a docile bird that she had screamed and fallen back towards the sink, lost her footing and landed on the floor.

The seagull, half running and half flapping its wings for take-off had reached the doorway to the kitchen, and taking advantage of an empty lounge had attempted to get airborne. It flew straight down the passageway and past Nev and Rock as they arrived at the foot of the ladder. When it reached the dead-end, the seagull collided with the wall, knocked over a small waist-high bookcase and landed in a pile on the floor between a copy of *'Men Are From Mars And Women Are From Venus'* and, appropriately enough, *'Jonathan Livingston Seagull'*.
Pausing only to compose its feathers, and

alarmed by Gasmark's "Catch that bird!" it found flight again and careered back into the lounge, gaining what little height there was to be had in the space available and making its way back in a blind panic to the kitchen where it smashed into the Venetian blinds.

At this point Gasmark leapt over the table, lunging towards the bird as it flapped manically in the sink before stumbling out onto the draining board and running across the work surface and falling down onto the floor. Nev had grabbed a cushion and was advancing, so too was Rock but they fell back as it came at them with beak snapping, and by the time they recovered themselves it had taken up position at the far end of the lounge, breathing heavily. And that's where it remained for a few brief moments, head moving from one side to the other as it regarded the four humans with disdain.

"Open...the...door," Rock breathed through gritted teeth, fearing another attack was imminent.

"I can't," Nev responded from behind his cushion.

Then, from the kitchen, there came the unmistakable sound of the blind being drawn up and Sally threw open the window. To the seagull, the sudden black hole that had appeared in the wall was too much to resist and it shot threw the lounge and flew like a bullet out into the night with a final, triumphant caw-caw and was gone.

With the gull gone, all four of them collapsed onto the floor. It was left to Nev to break the tension. "Well, I thought that went well."

*

The flat had taken a few hits, but on the whole it hadn't suffered too much at the hands of the seagull in its terrified bid for freedom. A standard lamp had fallen, crushing the lampshade and the bulb had smashed, the Venetian blind in the kitchen looked like someone had twisted it out of shape, some of the cushions that Gasmark and Sally had used to defend themselves from the lethal beaks were ripped where the bird had attacked and there were a liberal amount of stray feathers to pick up but as far as Sally was concerned their deposit was safe.

Nev picked up the cushions, Rock stood the lamp back up and straightened the dented lampshade as best he could. In the kitchen, Sally stood on a stool and reached across to straighten up the blinds.

Noticing paper strewn across the floor, Gasmark bent to scoop them all up. It was only when he looked at them that he realised they were doodlings Sally had been making: half-baked logo ideas, slogans - some of which were crossed out, some with ticks by them. One that caught his eye was a clever pastiche of the Happy Eater logo that featured the head of a seagull with its beak open surrounded by a circle. The circle then morphed into a wing that came round to point into the open mouth.

He was staring at it as Sally came into the lounge with four mugs of tea.

"Refreshment for the troops," she announced.

Gasmark held up the papers, "Flock au Van, Gullps, Seagrill...What's all this?"

"I've been reading up on the psychology of food," she replied, handing a mug to Gasmark. "I mean, realistically, who's gonna want to eat seagull?"

"So we're back to square one?"

"No, no you're missing the point. We still *feed* them SEAGULL but we *call* it something else. Seaside Sizzlers, Beaky Burgers. Y'know, catchy."

"Can we get away with that?" he asked taking a mouthful of tea.

"Why not? In business it's called Re-branding."

"She's got a point," Nev said in support, " Happens all the time."

9

It had all sounded so straightforward, compared to the previous, disastrous attempt. Rock had made three portable traps that he insisted would increase the amount of birds they could catch. There was low cloud cover and it was no way as hot as it had been on the previous attempt. Plus they also thought they now had, thanks to their experiences with the getaway bird in the flat, the true measure of their quarry.

The only thing that brought the success of the whole venture into question was the disguises Nev had suggested they adopt. And now, as they stood in the alleyway shrouded by shadow so no one would see them, Gasmark voiced his discomfort with what Rock had brought for them to wear.

"No. No way. I'm not going to do it dressed like this. No!"

"Calm down," said Nev in a hoarse whisper, attempting to pour water on his angst, "it's not a fashion parade."

"That's okay for you..." Gasmark complained, raising his hands to make his point and feeling four more arms join in his gesticulation, "you're not dressed as a fucking octopus."

This much was true. Rock's insistence that he could provide suitable disguises had actually materialized as costumes used to promote the

Shepway Life of Sea experience. And so he stood as a Seagull and Nev as a penguin.

"It was all I could borrow," Rock explained. "It was either that or a Lobster. And I thought that'd make you look like a total prick."

Gasmark was furious in his humiliation, "And I don't like this?" Nev was not to be diverted.

"Let's just be professional about this, shall we?"

"I still don't understand why we have to wear costumes."

"Do you want your face to be splashed all over those CCTV cameras?" Nev explained, before adding plainly, "And they're not costumes, they're disguises."

At which point Rock cut in, "Look, the quicker we get this done the better…and if anyone does see us, they'll probably think we're just students dicking about. It's perfect cover."

Gasmark, resplendent in a bulbous blue Octopus body complete with eyes and beak felt backed into a corner. It was two against one, and besides Rock was right, no-one in their right minds would think what they were about to do was anything other than students having a laugh. Begrudgingly he said, "Come on then, let's get on with it."

*

Barry thought he'd seen everything during his time as a security guard, but now, as he sat watching the bank of closed circuit television monitors in the Council offices he realized the folly of such complacency.

The small room was hot and sticky this evening, and he felt uncomfortable in his uniform as his shirt stuck to his frame. His forehead was dotted with droplets of perspiration and his hands felt clammy.

He reached forward taking a slurp out of his bottle of Coke and then returned to his snack, stirring the noodles round in the pot as he cast a weary eye over the monitors that flickered in front of him.

For the duration of his shift he had watched the towns' residents as they went about their business. Couples walking hand in hand on their way home. Arguments, break-ups, reconciliations, the odd drunk surreptitiously relieving himself behind a hedge. He had guided some of the cameras with a joystick and had even caught the tramp on a number of cameras as he wandered aimlessly through the streets, but what suddenly came up on a screen from a camera watching the beach almost made him spill his Pot Noodle.

"What the...?"

He thought he had just seen a man-sized seagull scuttle out from the shadows and across the field of view and disappear again out of shot. Putting the Pot Noodle to one side he leaned forwards, eyes scanning all the other monitors for the follow-on image, but there was nothing.

He scratched his head, unsure of what he'd seen.

Just when he had convinced himself that he hadn't seen a giant seagull galumphing across the screen an equally out-sized octopus scuttled into view, tentacles flailing and carrying what looked like...yes it was...a seagull.

Looking over his shoulder he called out to his partner on the graveyard shift, "Clive! Clive! Come and take a butchers at this!"

There was the sound of flushing, and then a fat balding man appeared in the doorway, tucking his shirt into the waistband of his trousers.

"What's up?"

"I dunno," he said pointing at one monitor and then another, "There...look...and there!" The screens were alive with frantic movement. First a penguin, then an octopus, then the large seagull, and then a flurry of feathers. The octopus holding a fishing net had lost it's footing and sprawled out on the shingle; a seagull was flapping its wings manically as it chased some ordinary-sized herring gulls towards the penguin who was holding what looked to the two security guards like a homemade lobster pot.

"What are they doing?"

As the guards dissolved into fits of laughter at the antics on the screens, they failed to see a group of teenagers caught on camera, leaping up and down on a climbing frame on the seafront, pulling pieces off and throwing them at each other. And if they had looked harder, they would also have seen a tramp trapped underneath the frame, being taunted at and pelted with clods of earth and their scrunched up cans of lager.

Clive was laughing fit to burst, "What do they look like?" Barry was joining in, pointing at the screen, "And that...what is that, a squid?"

For Barry the sudden unexpected exertion of sustained laughter was too much. Years of a sedentary lifestyle and fast food diet suddenly came home to roost. His chest tightened and his laughing hollowed out into a rasping sound. His fingers clawed at his collar to loosen the tie that was beginning to feel like a garrote.

The chair gave way as he slid off onto the floor, clutching his arm. The violent movements made Clive turn his head, and when he did so, he saw his partner's face turn a ghostly grey.

"Barry? Barry, mate?".

The gurgled reply from the floor turned his blood cold and he leaned across automatically to pick up the internal phone and dial 999.

"Ambulance!" he yelled.

10

Still in costume, Gasmark, Rock and Nev were a united band of brothers singing out of tune as they made their way triumphantly back home. Over their shoulders were black dustbin liners full of their prize catches. Rock's Gull-o-tines had delivered in spades and now they celebrated the only way they knew how: in song, with Gasmark taking the falsetto lead. "

Big gulls…they don't fry-eye-eye".
and Rock and Nev harmonizing with an off key,
"They don't fry".
"Big gulls…don't fry".
"Who says they don't fry?"

They were homeward bound and drunk on success.

Gasmark would have been the first to acknowledge that although he had felt ridiculous in the costumes Rock had provided for disguise, the evening had exceeded his expectations. The dead weight in his bag alone confirming that their venture was now well and truly under way.

The real test would come in the next few days when Sally's flyers - substituting for those for the *Shepway Life of Sea* that Rock was handing out - began to have an impact on trade and pointed people in the direction of his van. Then and only then, when they had impartial customers queuing up to buy their new food, would he know for sure whether the venture had wings.

They arrived at the flat and Nev put his finger up to his lips as he turned the key in the lock. The other two sniggered as they tiptoed across the threshold, carrying their bags.

In the darkness they looked like conscientious burglars who had undergone a change of heart and returned to the scene of the crime with the items they had stolen.

Once in the kitchen all three emptied their bags onto the table and stood back to marvel at the small mound of birds Rock's gull-o-tines had catch.

"Not a bad nights work, all-in-all," Nev said, stepping out of his costume, "so what's next?"

Gasmark reached across and picked up a bird by its legs so that the wings flopped down over its head. Not for the first time was he struck by just how big a herring gull actually was...close up.

"We pluck it!" he said and tossed the bird across to Rock and then did the same with anoher bird to Nev who made a considerable meal of catching it.

With all three of them now holding a dead bird there was only one thing for it.

"Keep a firm hold of the bird and pull the feathers away from the body like so..." and gave a quick, firm yank at some breast feathers which came away neatly in his hand. "Simple!"

Nev, who pulled a single feather from a bird by the living or dead, looked at the carcass in his hand, "This'll take hours," he said with a growing sense of dread for what was to come.

Gasmark looked up from his own bird which

was now beginning to show naked flesh even after a few hearty plucks, "Then you better get started."

*

Across the other side of town in her bedroom, Sally stirred, slightly aware that Rock still wasn't back. But before she could register it further she turned over and fell back into the dream she was having without a second thought.

When the alarm went off a few hours later, she found she was already awake. A hand stretched out to Rock's side had touched upon the cold side of the mattress. Rock hadn't come to bed.

She was not a morning person. She always felt at her lowest in those first few hours of the day with the prospect of another day stretching out just like the one before it, and the one before that and so on, that she became maudlin, depressed and frustrated.

Her life in Folkestone had flat lined. Her relationship with Rock was on the wane, and her career prospects outside of Gasmark's burger van were becoming less and less optimistic as the weeks went on.

Every day inevitably brought another rejection from another job application; and everyday, it seemed, another nail in her prospects. Gasmark, she knew, wore his despair on his sleeve whereas she balled it up inside, unable to express her frustrations to Rock because he was actually part of the problem.

Heaving herself up onto she ruffled her hair

and stretched out one last time before throwing the duvet off and getting up. With a slow yawn, she took down her shower robe from the hook on the back of the door and turned the handle.

By the time she stepped from the shower and reached for her towel, the hot water had pummeled away the usual early morning rough edges and the steam had softened her anxiety.

Looking into the mirror, she wiped away the fragile coating of condensation across its surface and regarded her reflection. She always had to fight to remind herself of the public face she presented to the world a face that belied none of her problems. It was almost as if it were a false canvas. She smiled at herself mockingly before sticking her tongue out at her reflection like a naughty child.

It was true that she'd enjoyed working on new logos and slogans for Gasmark's new venture. The rebranding, she felt sure, would work so long as they'd managed to catch enough birds this time. However it was just as possible to fall flat on its face.

The walk home in the early morning had done wonders for Rock's perspective. His gull-o-tines had made light work of the job of trapping the gulls. Nev and Gasmark couldn't have done it without him. Infact, in all probability they'd still be out there on the beaches impotently running after the birds in a vain attempt at capture; just like they had done previously.

With each step he took the pride in his creations grew. But why stop there? Why not try something that had always been nothing more tangible than a faraway dream. The older he got, the further away that dream had become. Until now, right here on this bank and shoal of time. The realisation made him stop in his tracks as if he'd suddenly had a veil removed from his eyes.

He had always wanted to fly.

His long cherished dream of flight had been with Rock for as long as he could remember. It had driven him from the clumsy construction of Airfix models with glue-coated fingers as a schoolboy, through the building of gliders to a half-baked desire to study Engineering at Brunel University that had only lasted a year before he'd dropped out.

What followed, as he spiraled in free-fall, was a series of jobs that held neither permanency nor interest. Call centre jobs selling insurance, data-input jobs found by temp agencies, more call centre jobs fielding calls on a fault line for a cable TV company, and sundry week-long 'engagements' which had all succeeded in only one thing: to confirm his worst fears that 'proper work' didn't suit him.

Eventually life had got in the way and his dreams of unaided flight had fluttered away, coming to rest in the corners of his mind where they began to gather dust.

Sally, then fresh out of University with her

sparkling degree and glittering future, had seemed an unlikely partner. Everyone had said so, but that made the pair of them even more determined to stay together. They had burned brightly, laughed loudly and gorged on life. It was only when her bright future dimmed and his prospects failed to take off did the laughter spread out and the doubt seep in.

They left their life in Norwood Junction and moved to the coast. "Relocating," Sally had announced grandly as they headed in a hired van down the M20 towards Folkestone. Rock had embraced the new start, but very quickly it had soured and become a drudge.

He had tears in his eyes as he found himself standing on the beach looking at the rising swell of the sea. The dream of flight returning to him like a long forgotten memory suddenly rediscovered.

The names of all the great aviators began to arrive swirling round in his head: Bleriot, the Wright Brothers, Lindbergh, and Earhart. And then suddenly, out of nowhere, a new name flew in, unbidden like a gatecrasher at the party and made him look up at the watercolour sky that was only now beginning to show streaks of light: Daedalus.

His past suddenly split wide open, and there he was - a timid child staring in wonder at a painting of the flight of Icarus. The very moment his fascination with unaided flight was born. The body arching upwards, aiming towards the open blue sky, the wings with their myriad of feathers each one painted with individual precision as if they had actually been plucked from a real bird and stuck on the page with glue...the glorious moment that man truly flew.

For Rock the moment of clarity was almost too much to bear. He had been living a life of frustration for what seemed like an eternity when all the time the answer was yelling at him from as far back as childhood: build...a pair...of wings.

Don't just dress up as a bird...*be* a bird. All he needed was feathers, and right now he knew exactly where he could get an unending supply.

Turning on his feet he began retracing his steps to Nev's flat.

*

Sally's first thought as she entered the kitchen was that something had fallen through the ceiling. There were lengths of wood on the table and mounds of feathers on the chairs and floor that wafted in little eddies with the slightest breath of wind.

Rock, in a pair of shorts and T-shirt stood amongst the sea of feathers.

"What the hell's all this?" she demanded, folding her arms. She could feel resentment rising.

"A project of inspiration", Rock announced proudly.

"A what?"

"It suddenly came to me while we were plucking the birds we'd caught. All those feathers and we still can't fly."

Sally looked at him as if he'd gone mad, "What are you talking about?"

She could not quite believe what she was hearing - or seeing for that matter. It had all become too surreal, especially this early in the morning to be confronted with a kitchen that now resembled an explosion in a mattress factory.

Far from being inspiration it had all the hallmarks of a mental breakdown.

"Have you been up all night?", she began, trying to put it all together, but was distracted by the welcome sound of post arriving. It provided her with a time-out card. "Hold that thought", she announced turning towards the hallway.

By the time she returned, Rock had begun rolling up his hastily drawn sketches and designs and was wrapping a rubberband around them.

Sally was sorting through the small collection of envelopes which she tossed into the bin one-by-one, "Junk. Junk. Junk...", before coming to a white envelope. Turning it over, she ran a thumb under the flap and pulled out the letter.

"Dear Ms. McIntyre, Thank you for your application for the post of PR and Marketing Assistant. Unfortunately...yah-de-yah-de-yah."

The day had delivered its aching misfortune again. She scrunched the letter in her hand, and held it to her chest.

"And junk."

Rock looked at her for a moment. At her face

curtained by the long auburn hair that covered her features as her head bowed in defeat. Before he could find some words to comfort what he knew would come next, her shoulders began to shake. A sob caught in her throat as she looked up, fire in her eyes, and waving the letter accusingly.

"Doesn't this get to you, living on the edge all the time?"

It was at this moment he chose the exactly the wrong words to say: "Lexxie says that if you're not living on the edge you're taking up too much space."

For Sally this was a tipping point. The key had turned and the floodgates broke open.

"Lexxie says," she mimicked, "What sort of crap's that? The only edge you're living on Rock is my bloody patience.
I'm sick of all this... breath holding. Shit jobs, shit lives going nowhere. It feels like I'm just stuck in a... in a..." and then it was just as if she became aware of the mess around her, "a fucking scrapyard! I thought we'd agreed you'd keep crap like this up in the loft."

Defeated by the situation, she tossed the letter on the floor and walked back through the lounge and back into the bedroom; slamming the door with as much force as she could. Moments later the familiar sounds of sobbing drifted faintly through to the kitchen as the letter gently unfolded itself on the floor.

11

The sun beat down from a cloudless sky and thanks to Sally's revamping of the van, it actually looked like an appealing place from which to buy food.

She was just erecting the Happy Seagull logo stand at the mouth of the lay-by and stood back to look at her handiwork. Unusually the morning had started well for her. Nothing from the postman to tarnish the day-to-come, and Rock had risen early and left for work while she was still in the shower, so there had been no crossed words.

Even the journey to work had filled her with a certain degree of happiness today. She put this down to the fact that, at grass roots level, she was beginning to do what she'd studied for at University; putting into practice all the theory she'd learnt. Inadvertently Gasmark had given her the very opportunity that countless companies, through their constant rejections, had steadfastly failed to do.

Even Gasmarkhad appeared happier at the challenge now facing them. By his own admission he had been resistant to the idea; didn't really think cooking seagulls was going to work, thought they would be too tough, taste too fishy, meat would be too dark, but since Horry had given the thumbs up, and the problem of stock purchase had been solved thanks to Rock's

Gull-o-tines, he had begun to see a break in the clouds of his despair. He'd even embraced Sally's idea that he wear a French-style toque, squashed at one side, which Sally had embroidered the legend: '*Cook me Quick - Eat me Slow!*' on the banded rim plus a red, white and blue neckerchief.

As Sally arrived back at the van, she waved here hand toward the tri-colouredbunting that skirted around the vans serving hatch.

"What do you think?"

Gasmark's wide smile gave her the answer well before he spoke, "Genius!"

"Really?"

"Really! I love it. You've got a real talent there, Sal," he said moving back inside the van.

"Yeah yeah yeah. Flattery'll get you somewhere," she said following him inside, keen to divert attention away from her endeavours,

"Right...is everything ready?"

"Yep."

"Seagulls?"

Gasmark opened the cooler and sitting there, nicely prepared and filleted sat a pile of what used to be seagulls.

"Check."

"Batter?"

"Check."

"Urn filled?"

"Check, check and triple check, Mon Petite General," and he clicked his heels and gave a quick salute.

Sally's smile matched his own, "Aha, you do speak French?"

Gasmark whipped out a 'Let's Speak Francais' pocketbook from his back pocket and smiled,

"Thought I'd make a start!"

"Great," Sally said and began the countdown to opening the hatch and seeing if all their hard work would pay off, "Okay - Ready - Three...two..." before Gasmark joined in at the end:
"...One...Lift-off!" and they leant across each end of the counter to push out the side flaps and opened the hatch.

Whatever they had been expecting, the actual view they got as they fixed the side supports in place took their breath away. Two coaches had just parked up and they were divesting themselves of a full compliment of passenger who were beginning to swarm out of the coaches.

Sally looked at Gasmark and with their mouths open their exchanged glances spoke volumes. As dream starts went, this was definitely in there with the medals. Gasmark rubbed his hands in a mixture of disbelief and expectation.

As they watched, however, it quickly became apparent that the crowd currently growing in number wasn't there for the food. Maps were produced and directions pointed and then, ant like in their uniformity, they began the trek across towards the white cliffs of Dover that stood like a distant beacon at the end of the curve of cliff from this starting point by the Martello Tower.

Sally and Gasmark were so focused on the receding rucksacks that they hadn't noticed the driver saunter over to the serving hatch.

"Bloody ramblers' parties. I 'ate 'em," he said, leaning on the counter, "Cuppa tea please, love."

"Yes sir," and as she turned away to take a Styrofoam cup from the packet and prepare the cup before adding the hot water from the urn she said, almost under her breath to Gasmark, "Did you really expect the feeding of the five thousand on the first day? You've got to let word get around. Trust me."

And almost on cue, the driver nodded at the blackboard erected outside the van, "An' what's this Euro Poulet then?"

Sally shot a look at Gasmark as if to say, "*Told you*" before launching into a pre-rehearsed sales patter.

They had spent many hours throwing possible names for the seagulls that hid the fact that they were infact just that. Seagulls would carry too much negative baggage, the name had to go, but what would work in its place? What name would create in the consumer a reassurance that would bring them flocking to the van which in itself had undergone a name change?

Ever since he had taken it over, Gasmark had traded under Gasmark's Grub but Sally argued that it sounded flat, uninspired, a real turn-off for prospective customers. What he needed was something that sounded fun, bright and inviting and so it became '*Gasmark's Gourmet Goodies*'.

As usual, Gasmark had required persuading, but for Sally, this was Year One, Term One of her Business Studies degree, "It's perfect. It contains the chefs' name, mixes Gourmet and Low Brow, is alliterative and employs the rule of three. I think you'd go a long way before you found something as bang on the money as that...and after all, it's the name of the business not the product. How're you getting on with ideas?" And so they'd trawled through various names: SeaGrill, Beaky Bites, WingWings before they'd agreed on Euro-Poulet. It acknowledged the chicken flavour while embracing the Continent, which would hopefully explain the slightly fishy tang.

It appeared to do the trick on the coach driver as he tucked in. Sally and Gasmark held their breaths as he worked his way through it. By the time he returned to the counter for another can of Coke he was all smiles.

"It might be foreign," he said appreciatively, "but it's certainly not muck. I tell you what, by the time those ramblers return they'll have worked up an appetite. If you're still open by the time they come back I'll point 'em in your direction and you'll be quids in."

And so they did. By the time the coach had loaded up its rambling cargo once more and pulled away, Gasmark had some good news for Sally as he checked the cool box: "We've shifted pretty much all the stock we started out with this morning."

"What did I tell you?" Sally said, adding up the days taking, "We're on our way. We're on our fucking way!"

*

If one business was busy taking off, then another was beginning to look very much dead in the water.

In the centre of the room an open coffin was laid out on the table like a large forgotten piece of cutlery. The curtains were drawn casting a dull gloom on the casket and the still body of Albert Lafferty resting inside it in a state of eternal grace.

Nev was circling the table while two grieving relatives remained at he door watching him.

After a couple circuits of the casket he stopped at the foot end and lifted up both arms, stuck his right out at forty-five degrees then formed a makeshift square with the thumb and forefinger of each hand and squinted through it as he would do a lens and imitated a zoom in and a zoom out.

"It's, I dunno, lacking something at the moment. Maybe if we can get the deceased to... y'know..." and he reached over into the coffin and tweaked the cheeks a little, pulling them in an upward curve, "Smile?"

The woman in the doorway turned into her husbands shoulder.

Sensing that he had probably overstepped the mark, Nev attempted to back track. Resting on his haunches so that he was below the lip of the coffin, he again adopted the makeshift camera with his hands and slowly raised himself up again. In his minds eye he would be able to create the same level of suspense as Spielberg had used when he kept the camera at water level in '*Jaws*'.

"Tell me," asked Nev absently, "Are they all his own teeth?"

This time the husband, separating himself from his wife's mourning grip said, "I think we've changed our minds. We're not going to want Dad's funeral filmed after all," and handed back the business card Nev had given them on his arrival. "If you could shut the door on your way out."

Before Nev could make any reply, or offer a twenty-five per cent discount, the couple turned away leaving Nev alone with the corpse.

"Another one bites the dust," he said. Then looked at the old man lying in the coffin, "Not that you need any reminding, eh?" he said forlornly.

Albert Lafferty just smiled.

12

Business, which had started a few short days ago with a coach driver and soon picked up with the ramblers returning from the White Cliff Walk had continued to go from strength to strength.

With each successive day a small queue had formed by the van and both Sally and Gasmark were properly, continuously busy for the first time. There was no time for idle chat and dreaming which ordinarily made up most of their day, but perhaps the biggest change they both discovered was customer satisfaction.

No one had turned up their noses, brought the food back or complained outright about what was being served up. Seagulls were clearly what they wanted to eat even if they didn't know it. With Euro-Poulet, however, they did know...and not only ate it, but also kept coming back for more.

"I told you it would pick up. Just takes time for word of mouth to get around," Sally said as they sashayed round one another, each serving a different customer.

Gasmark, handing over a polystyrene tray with chips and some deep fried seagull to another eager customer, beamed, "What did I say, you're a genius, Sal..." as her customer also left, leaving them momentarily alone, he took advantage of their sudden proximity and took her face in his hands, "...a genius!"

Before either of them could act on the closeness, they were interrupted by the authoritative cough of someone clearing their throat and demanding attention.

"Ahem!" It was Leonard Fowler, and he had chosen this day to make an unannounced inspection.

Sally had noticed the way he had loitered, always at he back of the queue until now, as the immediate rush for food had dissipated for the time being. But now as he stepped forward, looking up over and across the counter at the two of them he seemed to grow in stature.

"Euro Poulet?" Gasmark asked, misreading all the signs of officialdom. Fowler fished into his inside pocket and produced his identification,

"Fowler, Environmental Health."

"Environmental Health?" Gasmark visibly blanched and felt his throat dry and constrict. In all the time he'd been running the van he had never been visited by anyone from Environmental Health and Licensing. Initially he thought that it was only a matter of time but as the months went by he had begun to believe that it was actually because his lack of customers meant that there was a large possibility that the van wasn't actually at risk of contamination by bacteria. Clearly this was not the case, but the idle thought had made him smile. A smile that was now slipping like cooling wax on a candle.

Fowler sensed Gasmark's unease, and pressed

his advantage.

"Routine check to make sure you're complying with the food hygiene regulations," he explained, placing emphasis on *'complying'* and *'regulations'* and reveling in the effect they had,

"Now, if you'd just wash your hands before you touch any more food, we can begin the inspection."

Gasmark shot a worried glance at Sally as Fowler moved round the side of the van to the door and mounted the steps, ducking slightly as he entered.

"Mind your head," said Sally helpfully pointing towards a sign above the doorframe. Fowler nodded and stepped to one side where he ran a finger across the work surfaces, again more for intimidation than anything else.

"You'd be surprised the amount of germs we carry about in our hair alone," he said. This seemed to be aimed at Sally, although she didn't rise to it, so he merely said, "Surfaces clean..." and noted it down on his notepad. The rest of the office had gone paperless, and fully embraced tablet technology - a move driven by the self-proclaimed 'Tech Head', Ashley, but Fowler had resisted all attempts to drag him into the modern age and stuck steadfastly with pen and paper on which to make his initial reports.

It was bad enough that he had been forced into submitting them as word-processed documents without giving up the ink as well. Besides, he could wield a pen with such threat as

to render restaurateur putty in his hands.
He turned his attention next to a tray of prepared seagulls.

"Now, this is Euro Poulet is it?" he said looking over it as a vulture might its prey.

Gasmark seemed transfixed, rabbit-like in Fowler's headlight stare and could only manage an, "Er..."

Fortunately for him Sally stepped in, "That's right...would you like to try some? There's Southern Fry, Tikka, Coronation, Hot Chilli..." Fowler was unfazed by what he correctly perceived as an attempt to drive him from the task appointed him by Her Majesty, "Not until I'm satisfied of its origin. What are they? Not chicken, they're too big."

Gasmark panicked and blurted out, "French Chicken."

"What?"

Again Sally came to the rescue, "It's a translation."

"Where does it come from?"

"France!" Gasmark said before Sally could take control of the conversation.

Fowler cast a sceptical look at Gasmark who was standing stiffly with a spatula in his hand looking like a life size ventriloquist's dummy. As Fowler looked at him querulously, Gasmark waved the spatula and affected a smile that only reinforced the appearance of a mannequin.

"Fresh off the ferry every morning."

"And you can prove that? Invoices, delivery

notices and so forth?" Fowler persisted.

"Of course we can," reassured Sally, crossing her fingers behind her back out of sight of Fowler, "They're not here, obviously...but we can supply them if need be."

"How are they stored?" he continued, "And prepared... and cooked?" He moved closer to the storage area and Sally and Gasmark edged round to give him space. It appeared like the Tarantella in slow motion. Gasmark caught Sally's eyes. She just shrugged and continued, trying not to appear under any undue pressure, "Storage... over here."

Fowler was thorough, methodical and precise in his inspection. Fortunately for Gasmark, his own mild variation of OCD had for the first time paid dividends and the Environmental Officer was placated. By their very nature roadside vans providing a quick burger and a chipped mug of tea were not usually the cleanest places and more often than not Fowler's recommendations for improvement on a first visit ran over many pages, but in this case, *Gasmark's Gourmet Goodies* fared much better and as he walked from the van he was quietly impressed by the level of hygiene displayed. What concerned him more was the food being sold.

Euro Poulet.

It all sounded so plausibly European but at the same time something about it rang an alarm bell deep within him. He had learnt long ago that if something felt wrong, then it invariably was. Quietly he resolved to look into it.

Behind him in the van Gasmark and Sally were glad to see him go.

"That wasn't too bad, was it?"

Gasmark was less confident, "What about those invoices?"

"No problem...I'll run something up on the computer. He'll never know the difference."

"Still, he'll be back."

Sally was mildly put out by Gasmark's pessimism, "Oh come on, why should he be?" Gasmark's logic was straightforward: "They're as bad as rats, Environmental Health. Once they start sniffing about, there's no getting rid of them. Especially one like that. Y'know what they say? The only good Health Inspector..." he stated, raising his forefinger and pretending to shoot the retreating civil servant, "...is a dead one," before blowing across the top of his finger as if the smoking barrel of a gun.

*

The bandstand on the Leas Cliff was silent. The red and white striped deck chairs that during the day were fanned out around the bandstand for the comfort and convenience of holidaymakers who sat and listened to the brass band were now cleared away and stacked up under a lean-to.

Now, as the sun dipped low on the horizon and gave the appearance of actually touching the

English Channel, the ghosts of the music produced during the daily performances by the Folkestone Brass Players drifted through the bandstand where Rock, dressed in his seagull costume, was being chased by Lexxie. Both were laughing with the release caused by the end of another working week.

As Lexxie got closer Rock flapped his wings and leapt into the air mocking flight. This was met with further gales of laughter from his working partner who stopped chasing to catch her breath.

"C'mon, it's easy. Just do it!" Lexxie shook her head, taking in great lungfuls of air

"No no, stop! I can't keep up!" and collapsed with laughter on the wooden bandstand floor.

Rock grinned. These days spent with Lexxie were fun and argument free. A pleasant reminder of better times he used to share with Sally.

*

Apart from the interlude supplied by Fowler's Environmental Health visit, the day had otherwise been a full one for Gasmark and Sally. It had proved unequivocally that cooking was what Gasmark wanted to do with his life.

He had found, in these few short hours, that the smiles on the faces of satisfied customers upon receipt of something he had created lifted his spirits like nothing had done in Folkestone since he'd arrived and been held up at water-filled gunpoint.

The till, the very object in the van which had been quiet for so long, had finally found its voice and fairly sang its way through the day as it opened and closed. And it was now only silent because Gasmark had left it open while he cashed up the days takings. The takings were so good infact, that it was Gasmark's turn to sing, which he did with a broad smile on his face:

"Zank 'eavens for little gulls, for little gulls get eaten every day. Zank 'eavens for little gulls, zey get eaten in the most delightful way."

"Someone's happy", Sally observed as she came back into the van with the sauces left out on the picnic tables. Gasmark finished counting the notes and then rolled them up before wrapping a rubber band round them and placing them on the counter next to the till.

"With good reason," he said, "Here," and folded a few notes that he had kept over which he handed over to Sally.

"What's this?" she asked.

"Wages, plus back pay - y'know, for everything else."

"Oh, Gasmark. Thanks," she said and reached up to peck him on the cheek.

All the time the business had been soaring there was an unseen tension. A blot on their landscape. And at the exact moment of elation with the best ever takings Gasmark had ever seen for the van there came the familiar sound of an approaching Jaguar and almost immediately his balloon of happiness popped.

Looking out of the van through the serving hatch he saw the car door open and Lenny, dressed to kill in black tie and tuxedo, holding a bouquet of roses, stepped out. Drawing himself up to his full height, he straightened the bow tie, loosening it a touch which suggested such wear wasn't an often occurrence, and walked towards the van.

"Hey Gobshite!" he called out. His harsh Glaswegian accent grating in the air.

"Gasmark."

Lenny ignored Gasmark's repeated correction of his name.

"I don't know what it is," he said, ducking into the van, "but I just seem to be drawn here."

"Got a date?" Sally asked, folding her arms protectively. This tall, aggressive gangster made her skin crawl, but at the same time brought out the combative side of her nature, "Who's the unlucky lady?"

Lenny smiled. He knew his height and comportment gave him power, and he took Sally's aggression in his stride, "I thought I'd make you an offer you cannae refuse. Dinner for two at a nice little Bistro I...have an interest in," he said handing over the flowers. But she remained resolute.

"You're not my type," and placed them on the counter.

Lenny moved in uncomfortably close to Sally in the confines of the van.

"Oh I think I am. It's just a matter of time 'til you admit it."

It was then he spied the rolled notes standing besides the open till.

"What have we here? Business pickin' up at last is it?" He reached across, picked up the roll and tossed it in the air, "Very tasty."

"No, that's..." began Gasmark, terrified at the thought of losing all his takings in the shape of back-payments, but yet again Sally came to the rescue and plucked it out of the air before it could land in the Glaswegian's palm,

"...mine!" she said, "Deposit for a new flat."

Before anything more could be said, she stuffed it deep in her pocket and challenged Lenny to contradict her. But he remained impassive, giving nothing away as to whether he believed her or not. Instead he turned his attention back to Gasmark who he backed into a corner.

"All right," he said levelly, "but if I find out you're pulling a fast one... you'll wish very hard that you'd never been born. Both of youse! Understand me?"

They both nodded, "Yes Lenny."

"Well make sure ya do, 'cause I'm not known for my sense of humour. Right?" he warned as he turned to the door, not seeing the warning sign above it that Sally had previously pointed out to Fowler.

"Lenny..." Sally said at what she hoped was exactly the right moment. His head turned just enough for him to miss the sign and as he continued forward he cracked the top right-hand side of his balding head against the door jam, and recoiled as the instant pain swept over his cranium like a lightning bolt. As the pain drained away his eyes opened and fixed on Sally as if momentarily considering a violent outburst, but saw her extending the bouquet of roses, "Don't forget your flowers."

"Keep 'em," he spat thunderously and ducked out of the van.

The silence left by Lenny's departure was broken only by the revving of the Jaguar as it roared away.

Gasmark let out a sigh of relief, "Sally to the rescue again, eh?"

She fished in her pocket and drew out the roll of notes and waved them teasingly towards him,

"At this rate, you're going to have to make it up to me." But before either of them could react, she reached for her jacket and shoulder bag, "But not tonight, I've got things to do. Another time, eh?" and twirled out of the van.

Gasmark ducked a little to watch her through the serving hatch and let his stomach tingle. Pushing the feeling aside he called out, "Yeah, I'll finish up here. See ya!"

13

The postbox had been well chosen. Sally had decided that this application for a job with European connections required a postbox that faced the Continent. It would, she felt, be a good omen. So when she remembered the postbox built into the wall of the churchyard she passed everyday on her way up to the Martello Tower and Gasmark's van, she knew she had found her postal talisman; and this was where she was heading with the application form nestling in her shoulder bag as she made her way down from the cliff-top into the old town by the harbour and then up a sloping path that led directly to the churchyard.

In the churchyard itself, the council had long ago insisted on a litterbin, and for Horry it was perfect, incontrovertible proof that there was a God. Of all the bins scattered in and around Folkestone, this was the one that could regularly be relied upon to supply provender.

"Manna from Heaven," he often joked, mainly to himself, as he tucked into the leftovers he'd gratefully retrieved from the bin. This evening was no exception and he pulled out a bundle of chip papers with a wink skywards to the

Almighty. As he unwrapped the paper he paused to rub his hands. There, laid out on his lap, was a veritable micro-feast of a half-eaten Hake, a large fistful of chips and two thirds of a saveloy.

"Ah..." he announced grandly, "Dinner is served!"

Sally stood at the postbox with the Foolscap envelope resting upon her two upturned palms. It looked to the untrained eye as if she was weighing it, and in a sense she was. Weighing up her chances of a positive outcome; weighing up the possibilities of a '*Yes*' rather than another '*No*'; weighing up her future because right now, upon this bank and shoal of time she felt as if her whole life depended on it.

Being in the shadow of the church made her do something she hadn't done since Middle school: she said a short prayer. Having been so long since she uttered such things it wasn't an official prayer, the likes of which got said week-in, week-out inside the building but instead a hastily made up one that even once it was said aloud, smacked of desperation. She shook her head, angry with herself for seeking the guiding hand of a deity she didn't really believe existed.

"Listen to yourself McIntyre!" she chided out loud, "Just post the bloody thing." With a hasty look around her to ensure she wasn't being observed she quickly lifted the envelope to her lips, whispered, "Please come through," and kissed it before posting it through the dark waiting rectangled mouth of the postbox.

Her hands stayed on its lips for a while as she imagined its short journey to the foot of the interior and saw it waiting, patiently for the next pick-up that, according to the white plaque on the small door, was in fifteen minutes. Then, satisfied that there was nothing more she could do, she hitched the bag higher up on her shoulder, turned towards the churchyard and pushed open the gate.

Horry was making good progress through his evening feast as Sally closed the gate and walked towards him sitting on the bench that neighboured the bin.

"Hi, Horry."

The tramp looked up, having popped the last of the saveloy in his mouth, and licked his lips,

"Just in time for the main course," he said and offered her a chip which she took as she sat beside him on the bench.

There they sat for a few moments, lost in thought. Across the pathway stood a statue of a winged angel, its hands outstretched and head bowed in supplication. The years and the elements had played their part of eating away at the stone masonry, but there she stood a witness to christenings, marriages and funerals down the decades. A lone seagull fluttered down to land on the angel's head.

The carved face smiled benevolently down on them. Sally noticed her as if for the first time and something inside her felt uneasy, almost as if the statue were telling her off for offering up a half-felt prayer for something as money driven as a career prospect. She looked away and in doing so noticed a crumpled travelled brochure in the process of escaping from Horry's overcoat pocket. She picked it up and looked at the photograph of a sun-kissed Hawaiian beach which beckoned the would-be traveller on a summer cruise, and read the text emblazoned on the front of the brochure:

"*Sail the Seven Seas*? You a sailor, Horry?"

He dropped a piece of the battered Hake into his mouth, much to the annoyance of the seagull who had been joined by another and together they threw their heads back and voiced their displeasure at not being allowed to join in with the meal.

"Was... once," he said.

"You like the sea then?" she asked, helping herself to another chip.

"Ooh yeah... You never lose sight of your dreams, not if you never take your eyes off the horizon." He picked the final chip out of the wrapping and tossed it across the path where it was intercepted in a flurry of feathers, by the two seagulls in a vociferous squabble of ownership, and angrily pulled at each end until it broke off, and the pair of birds flew up into the air each with their little piece of food. He then tore off a piece of the white paper and mimicked a serviette by dabbing the corners of his mouth to signify the end of the meal.

"Hold on a minute," Sally announced diving into her bag, "I've got...", and pulled out a bar of chocolate, "Dessert!" Breaking it in two, she passed half to Horry who took it.

"Well, if it'll help you out," he said and unwrapped the purple foil to reveal the chocolate beneath and they both ate in companionable silence.

14

The start of another working day was proving to be more than a refreshing change for the Environmental Health Officers gathered round Ashley's computer screen. He had been sent a video file of some CCTV footage that had been filmed a few nights before, when Barry had suffered his unfortunate heart attack that had landed him in the Royal Victoria Hospital, and was now sharing it with his colleagues.

They were enjoying it as much as he had the night before when he opened attachment. As the laughter enveloped them all, Ashley pointed at the screen - of someone dressed in a seagull costume scurrying around on the beach with all the elegance of a baby foal.

"Look…look, there…isn't that Steven Seagull?" he managed to say before collapsing into more laughter. Gridley, ever one to follow Ashley's lead pitched in, "No no…it's Bird Pitt!" which was met by more appreciative guffaws.

Behind the small group, some now having to lean on the desks to catch their breath and wipe their eyes the door opened and Fowler stepped in, removed his overcoat and placed it on the hook.

"Ah…the Birdman of Alcatraz!" someone said as the human seagull leapt at a real-life herring gull on the beach and missed. Ashley caught his breath, and looking round noticed Fowler had arrived and was doing his best to ignore them all as he slipped in behind his own desk across the room.

"Fowler,! Fowler you gotta see this..."

"What is it this time? A mousetrap that plays the National Anthem? Isn't it time you grew up?"

"No, no," Ashley corrected, "isn't this your lot - 'The undercover crack commandos ridding the town of our flying pests'. Who are they - The A-Team?"

"You mean the *Seagull Prevention Group*," corrected Fowler, determined to give the small working party set up to find a solution to the towns gull problem due recognition and not have it denigrated by the likes of Ashley and his guffawing clowns, "What about it?"

"Looks like *You've Been Framed. Where Seagulls Dare* we reckon, although' judging from the mess, it could just as well be the *Dirty Dozen*!" and again he fell into peals of laughter joined by the rest of the office.

This time Fowler's curiosity was piqued and he rose from his chair, looking at the screen.

"Where did you get this?" he asked, as he got closer.

"Contacts, mate. Contacts. One of the CCTV guys got it off the system a couple of nights ago."

Fowler stood impassive, oblivious to the hilarity around him, staring at the flickering video images of Nev, Rock and Gasmark in their fancy dress catching seagulls by night.

"Who...*are*...they?" he said almost to himself

as the Seagull, Lobster and Octopus leapt and dived and flapped and chased their way across the screen. Why would people want to catch seagulls? And, more importantly from a Health Inspector's point of view, what would they do with them once caught?

Transfixed he watched on, while all the others collapsed with laughter about him. Fowler's gaze became more serious as the questions led to only one possible answer: to eat; and this was very much where he came in. The only problem was going to be finding them so that he could bring the full force of the law down at their door. Fortunately, thanks to his involvement with the *Seagull Prevention Group*, he already had the means necessary. Turning away from the computer screen, a plan was already forming in his mind.

*

As the summer wore on, Gasmark's Gourmet Goodies proved anything but a flash in the pan. Word had got around that there was something special cooking up by the Martello Tower and day by day, more and more people turned up at the van to join the healthy queues. One thing that Sally was the first to notice was the considerable rise in returning trade. They were beginning to see 'regulars' facing them at the serving hatch.

The effect of this rise in custom meant longer nights catching the birds, but thanks mainly to Rock's Gull-o-tines the process wasn't half as difficult as it had appeared to be when they'd initially started the venture.

The problem of what to do with the rising mountain of feathers, which came off the plucked birds, had also been solved by Rock who quietly took the full to bursting bin liners away into the attic while at the same time refusing to say what he needed them for.

But Gasmark's success drew suspicious eyes, not least from Fowler who had taken to turning up at the security room with a large street map of the town and would spend hours scanning the CCTV images and marking the times and areas when the disguised seagull rustlers were at work. Slowly a pattern began to emerge, and for a man who felt most content with patterns of behaviour, Fowler plotted his next move with the precision of a military general, certain that he could catch these avarian malefactors without too much trouble.

According to Fowler's calculations tonight was a prime night for the gull rustlers to strike. The moon was a new one, which meant they would be shrouded by the dark much more than they would be by a bright, luminous moon at its fullest. The thinnest of crescents hung in the sky an impossible distance away.

Clouds skimmed the darkness above as a light breeze worked its way up the scale to a wind, and Fowler sat in the back of a transit van he'd requisitioned from the vehicle pool earlier in the evening checking his walkie-talkies that the SPG used to communicate with each other.

For tonight's assignment he had chosen just two members of the group: Madeleine Schnook an earnest woman from Scandinavia who shared his passion for order, and Derek Clancy whom Fowler had never seen in anything other than the faded blue anorak that he now pulled close to him.

Both were trusted members of the *Seagull Prevention Group*, and as such perfect for this extra mission. Madeleine twiddled the on/off switch on her walkie-talkie absent mindedly and suddenly let out a surprised yelp as it clicked on and emitted a searing drop of feedback for being so close to the other two devices in the van.

Fowler leant forwards. "As you know I've been observing the nocturnal movements of these...criminals for many weeks and I believe that I have discovered their modus operandi. I have been able, in the last few days, to predict exactly when and where they will strike and because of this I am confident that tonight we will be able to apprehend them red-handed." Both Schnook and Clancy nodded. This made perfect sense. If there was one thing they admired above all others in Fowler it was his fastidious attention to detail. They knew he was right. He continued with their briefing.

"You both have walkie-talkies," he paused to look at Madeline who reddened a little and instinctively pulled her hand away from the on/off button, "and street maps. I have highlighted the probable nesting area that will be targeted tonight with a green highlighter pen. I propose we fan out in a triangular pattern and once they begin their trapping we can call for back up. I have warned the local constabulary of the likelihood of a late night call to arms and am confident that we can wrap this whole thing up satisfactorily before the dawn."

He looked up again. This was an historic moment and he wanted his team to be aware of it. To his joy he found them positively beaming and if Derek Clancy could ever have been described as straining the leash, this was it. "Any questions?"

"Do we get a break?" Derek asked.

"A break?" Fowler repeated.

"Yes. I mean it's out-of-hours work, and I've brought a flask with some coffee in it, and my Mum's baked some flap-jacks."

Madeleine clapped her hands together, "I love flapjacks!" she interjected.

Fowler seemed momentarily lost for words. "Did they stop for a break during the D-Day landings?" he enquired, hoping that mention of the storming of Omaha, Juno and Gold might inspire them as well as instill in them the need to forego the usual work-time directives. "No they did not! And neither shall we until the job of apprehension is done. I chose you because you are the cream of the team and not jobsworths. I hope I haven't made an error of judgment?" He let the comment hang in the air, letting its weight settle on their consciences. Derek was the first to speak, "Well, put like that…" he said.

"Good!" announced Fowler, opening the rear doors, "then let's go."

Unfortunately for Fowler and his crack team, his calculations had proved too rigid and not taken into account the human factor, and just as the three of them were alighting from the transit van that had been parked beneath a flickering street lamp, Gasmark, Nev and Sally were leaving the pub after celebrating another successful days trading. Their freezers were packed so full with birds that another evenings catching would have meant a surfeit of stock, and so they had chosen to relax instead.

In blissful ignorance of the plans being hatched around them they walked past the flickering street lamp without so much a second glance at the poorly parked transit van, warm in the glow of an alcohol-fuelled revelry.

It was four o'clock by the time Fowler called time on the operation, and despite of his failure, and the gloom on his team, he found solace in the knowledge that Derek Clancy had a flask of hot coffee and flapjacks that he was keen to share. Sitting in the back of the transit van he wondered emptily if this was how the Allied Forces had spent the immediate hours after taking the beachheads in Normandy.

15

Nev had taken Gasmark's success as a sign. He was sure that some of the good fortune his flat mate was enjoying would rub off on his funeral filming enterprise. Although he had yet to bag another potential customer since the Hegley-Stone debacle, and had suffered knockback after knockback, he refused to give up the ghost. That was what brought him to the widow Muriel Edgware's over-furnished flat with his sales patter ready and polished.

The old lady sat at one end of the sofa gently stirring the sugar into Nev's tea as he pulled out his carefully prepared portfolios.

"Look, you don't want to pay for your funeral right now, Mrs. E," he said, opting for a slightly matey, conversational patter, "I understand that. Who would? But I can cut you in on a very tasty package that'll take away the worry."

"Can you, dear?" she said handing over the china cup and saucer with wobbling hand. "Care for a biscuit?"

Nev took it and placed it on the coffee table, eager to engage Mrs. Edgware in the sales possibilities of her own funeral.

While she had tottered off to the kitchen to make the tea, he had looked around her lounge and come to the conclusion that she didn't have a lot of disposable money. It also helped that her savings account book had lain open on the sideboard, and the numbers contained within hadn't pointed to a wealthy widow. With this in mind, Nev had begun to mentally alter his pitch to suit his client.

As Mrs. Edgware nibbled on a custard cream, Nev edged towards her on the sofa, the portfolio open on his lap.

"How about advertising space on the hearse?' he enquired. It was a desperate suggestion, and he watched as the idea hit a polite brick wall.

"I don't think so, do you dear?" Nev had to agree that it probably wasn't one of his better ideas, but his mind was too busy racing to find another solution in order to clinch the deal to take offence at her polite refusal.

"What if you considered selling your body to science?" he wondered aloud, "It's cash up front?"

But again the widow just shook her head. Nev took a sip of his tea. He had been shocked at the old lady's frailty and her vulnerability, and the more he continued the less he wanted to do anything other than the right thing by her. But his options were running out. It was then that he had a brainwave.

"How does the word '*sponsorship*' grab you?" Mrs. Edgware looked balefully up at him and he knew then that it was a lost cause.

"Would you like another cup of tea?" she asked.

Nev closed the portfolio in exasperation and slumped back on the sofa. She had won him over, and he couldn't bring himself to close the deal by any means necessary. Now it was his time to demur.

"I'm fine, Mrs. E," he said, "but I wouldn't say no to that biscuit."

*

The Amphitheatre on the Lower Leas coastal path was deserted by the time Gasmark and Sally strolled towards it. It wasn't Sally's usual route home, but the way her relationship with Rock was unraveling she felt no compunction to hurry home.

Gasmark had said he'd felt like a walk after being in the confines of the van all day, so he'd driven them both back to his flat, parked up and then accompanied Sally on her final part of the journey. Except the journey had turned into a meander and when they passed by an Off Licence, Gasmark popped in to buy some cans of lager without any disagreement from Sally.

Comfortable in each other's company, they had then wandered the length of the Leas and down the under-lit zigzag path that snaked its way towards the Amphitheatre with its seats carved out of the ground. There they settled, and Gasmark opened two of the cans, handing one to Sally as he leaned back on his elbows and looked out over the Channel.

"Twenty one miles to France," he said.

"Or 3,199 nautical miles - as the crow flies," Sally added taking a mouthful of lager.

"How do you know this stuff?" Gasmark asked

looking across at her. The slight breeze blew her auburn hair away from her face and he was reminded fleetingly of a slo-mo advert for hairspray. She shook her head a little feeling the hair lift in the breath of wind.

"I Googled it." She looked at Gasmark and then giggled, "What?"

"Nothing, it's just the way you store this stuff." She tapped the side of her head, "There's gold in them thar brain cells!"

"I love looking at the sea from up here, so still," he said. "On nights like this it could almost be made of glass."

"How did we do today?" Sally asked without turning to face him. Gasmark put his can down and reached into the pocket of his hooded jacket to retrieve the roll of notes.

"I haven't cashed up yet. I could do a rough tally now."

"By moonlight! Go on." she urged and lay back, as he flicked through the notes, counting rapidly under his breath as he did so.

Sally hadn't known Gasmark for long, but for all the brevity of their friendship - and given that he was, in effect, her boss - she never felt the need to speak to fill the silence. Which is why she gazed up at the early night sky, with its blue fading into a deep purple before becoming black and became lost in counting the slowly emerging stars.

There were nights she could remember shortly after they discovered the attic space had a hatch, when she and Rock used to climb out onto the roof of their flat with a blanket and lie there cut off from the world and spend all night making up names for constellations: *The Frying Pan. The Lobster. The Pince-Nez* and her favourite: *The Armadillo.*

The recollection brought her up short, and she sat up and took another swig of lager to wash away the memory.

"So..." she said, running a hand through her hair, "How did we do today, good?"

Gasmark had finished wrapping the rubber band round the notes again, and slid them back into his pocket, "Good? Better than good, Sal," he said raising the can to his lips, but pausing before he took a drink, "We did bloody fantastic!"

"How much we take?"

"Over three hundred and fifty quid."

Sally let her jaw drop. They had never taken anything approaching that before although; admittedly they had been climbing steadily. She let her open mouth stretch into the widest grin possible and leapt to her feet. With a whoop of unrestrained joy she reached across and dragged Gasmark to his feet. He was in the process of pulling open another can, and the sudden jolt was enough to unsteady him on his feet and he fell towards Sally. She took hold of him and together they danced round in wide, sweeping, celebratory circles. Their cries of joy filled the air of the Amphitheatre and swirled round them like newly freed birds.

Stopping for a moment, Gasmark placed his thumb over the cans opening and shook it vigorously before it away allowing the lager to froth and spray into the air to accompany the whelps of unfettered delight.

Whether it was the months of repressed unhappiness with her domestic situation, or the sudden realization of their depth of feeling she had for Gasmark, but Sally gave in to the moment, grabbed hold of his face and, pulling it towards her, kissed him hard on the lips.

Suddenly the moment froze, and as she released him she wondered whether she had crossed the line. Her answer came thick and passionately fast as he tossed the can aside and kissed her mouth with unrestrained passion.

From the second she had stepped into the van to explain how he operated the till and gone from being customer to employee, he had dreamt of this moment.

The days of burger hell had only served to fuel his desire for her, as she was the only bright light in an otherwise dark night of the soul in his struggle to come to terms with the fact that the business was, financially speaking, heading over the cliff. And it had been her business acumen that had navigated the turnaround in his fortunes. He had everything to thank her for, and more besides.

"Tell me one thing," he said, putting a temporary brake on their embrace.

"What?"

"Just to get things straight...you're only interested in me because of my money, right?" Her eyes twinkled and as she kissed him again, she teasingly bit his lower lip, "Absolutely!"

16

The morning arrived brilliantly bright and brilliantly blue from the moment the sun had risen. Gasmark knew this because he had seen it for himself.

Sally lay beside him wrapped in sleep, but Gasmark had slept lightly and now, as the dawn gave way to the first sounds of the summer day he was awake and drinking it all in. The breeze whispered in through the open window and swept a cooling tongue of air across the sheets on the bed.

He knew a line had been crossed but knew, deep down, that it wasn't a negative. Gone was his diffident old self to be replaced by a new, confident person. When Sally had kissed him last night for the first time he had not stuttered and made awkward excuses, but had grabbed the moment, grasped life and gone with his desire. He had come to a crossroads in his life and with that reciprocated kiss had taken the path that, for him, was the less travelled.

Now everything was changed. The light was brighter, the air tasted different. This was what it was like to be a winner. He could feel it instinctively.

Sally stirred but didn't wake.

Gasmark looked at her again and then pulled himself up slowly and cradled his head in the cupped hands behind him to reflect on events of last night.

They had hurried back to his flat, while the desire was still strong within them. Thanks to Nev's allegiance to football the flat was empty and Gasmark knew that once the match ended and the beer started flowing, they wouldn't be disturbed until much later.

As if seeing his room with fresh eyes, he looked at the floor across which was strewn, like a pathway to the bed with their clothes which had fallen as they had been removed in the journey to his bed. His body still tingled with the memory of Sally's touch and the sex that had followed.

He looked across at her sleeping frame and wondered 'What next?' Whether he liked it or not they had created a potential explosive situation with Rock that had to be dealt with in a mature and responsible manner befitting of the adults they were.

But not just yet.

He closed his eyes and drifted off into an untroubled sleep that was broken by Nev rapping on the door.

"Hands off cocks and on socks! You better move the van unless you want a ticket. You having a day off or what?"

Gasmark jolted awake and looked at the clock.

"Fuck! Sal...the time!" he said, half sliding off the bed in his disorientation.

She opened her eyes, and seeing him pulling his jeans on was immediately confused. But then she cast an eye in the direction of the digital clock radio to the right of the bed and the confusion was stripped away from her in an instant and she was suddenly wide-awake.

There was no time for pleasantries. She scooped up her clothes and perched on the end of the bed getting dressed, while Gasmark, a T-Shirt being pulled over his head, disappeared out of the room.

This, she suddenly realised, as the door swung shut and closed with a pin-drop click, presented her with a potentially embarrassing problem. Nev was still in the flat and to meet him across the hallway would inevitably lead to the kind of awkward situation she could well do without.

She chanced a look out of the window and saw Gasmark step out of the front door and make for the van. He was still barefoot, so his absence would be temporary. He clearly intended to just move the van before returning. She drew her hair back behind her head and fed it through a hair band she'd pulled from her trouser pocket. Then she quickly fluffed the pillows and pulled the duvet over the bed and smoothed its surface before sitting on the bed once more as she slipped her left shoe on and then looked around for the other one.

All the time she was playing through possible conversation scenarios that she could execute, and none of them sounded anything other than carefully worded variations of *"Morning Nev. I've just cheated on my boyfriend!"*

In frustration she thumped the duvet just as the door opened and Nev appeared holding a mug of tea and a plate of buttered toast.

"Breakfast?" he asked.

She looked blankly. Numb and incapable of speech. This was one scenario she hadn't considered, and as if to answer the unspoken question Nev chipped in with: "Your bag and coat were on the floor. And this..." he said dangling her missing shoe from his little finger, "had found its way onto the angle-poise. I sort of did the maths."

The moment seemed frozen. Not out of embarrassment or awkwardness - but just because neither of them knew who was going to make the next move.

As it turned out, it was Sally: "Morning Nev. I've just cheated on my boyfriend."

*

The rest of the day had been weird. Because of the rude awakening their unplanned lie-in had caused neither Sally or Gasmark had had time to talk about what had happened between them or what would happen next. Gasmark thought Sally would simply leave Rock and move in with him - at least that's what he wanted, but he was finding it hard to find the time to talk about it and didn't want their future together to be agreed as part of a snatched conversation between hungry customers.

For her part Sally was in turmoil. She knew that her relationship with Rock was if not dead then very near it but didn't know how to go about the next step. And was Gasmark the right step, or was he just the stepping-stone caused by her unhappiness with Rock?

And so the day proceeded with both of them dancing on emotional eggshells which led to each of them believing that the other was having second thoughts about what had taken place. It was something of a relief to be so busy, at least it provided an excuse not to sit down and talk about it.

Not just yet.

A group of youths in hoodies, carrying their skateboards had just been served, and were moving away in their group, dipping into a couple of shared cones of chips and separating out the Euro Poulet with a mixture of obscenities and laughter. Gasmark was scraping the hot plate with a spatula and Sally was wiping down the counter when a man dressed fashionably in designer clothes stepped forwards.

Nodding towards the sign he asked, "What's this Euro Poulet?"

Gasmark tensed, fearing another Environmental Health Officer, but Sally smiled confidently and put aside her Jay cloth.

"Straight off the ferry this morning. A European fowl prepared and cooked by our very own Galloping Gourmet. Very popular."

The man turned towards the retreating group of youths whose laughter could still be heard on the wind, "So it appears. Let's see what all the fuss is about then," he said, pulling out his wallet and smiling, "I'll have what they've had."

Once the food had been cooked and served, and the stranger paid, he retreated to the picnic bench that sat nearer the cliff-edge. The late afternoon was balmy, and the sky had faint wisps of cirrus cloud, which looked like they'd drifted off a carelessly held candyfloss, and the seagulls wheeled and swooped noiselessly giving them a surreal appearance. As if they were a mime playing out some elaborate narrative on the wind.

Gasmark busied himself in the van, rehearsing what he was going to say to properly break the ice with Sally. One wrong word, one unintentional gesture and the whole fragile house of cards would come crashing to the ground.

For her part, Sally had moved out towards the picnic bench as soon as she saw the curious stranger had finished his meal and was now engaged in a conversation with him. There was laughter, and as Gasmark looked up from drying his hands on a tea towel, Sally raised her right hand to her breast and was smiling. He immediately felt a twist in his own chest, shocked at the realization of how much he felt for her.

Almost on cue she looked up and without even pausing in her conversation, waved her fingers at him. The diner, wiping his mouth on a serviette followed her gaze momentarily. Sally then said something, picked up the polystyrene tray and smiled, before walking back towards him.

"He says compliments to the chef," she said tipping the tray into the bin by the door and climbing up into the van, "You're not going to believe this. Turns out he's a gourmet critic with a weakness for fast food. Says he's going to write a feature for the Sunday paper he writes a column for. Reckons it'll put us on the map." It was enough to change the whole mood in the van.

"On the map! Sal, one good review and we're made! *Egon Ronay* stars, entries in the *Good Food Guide*, the lot! I'll be a TV celebrity chef before you can say Heston Blumenthal! I can see it now..." he said spreading his hands out as if to conjure up the picture, "A kitchen set foregrounded by a work surface. Behind is a large glitzy sign: '*GASMARK LIVE FOR 30 MINUTES*'. And the off-screen announcer: '*Ladies and gentlemen, please welcome the star of the show... Heeeeeere's Gasmark!*' to wild audience applause."

He made the sound of what he hoped was wild audience applause and then stopped, suddenly aware that it was just the two of them in the van. No cameras, no studio lights or audience of adoring fans. He dropped his hands feeling foolish. Sally picked up the tea towel and flicked him with it playfully.

"You're a loony," she said, a smile dancing across her face. Reaching up on her toes she looped the towel round his neck and drew him closer, "but at least you're a happy loony," and

kissed him properly for the first time that day.
That, Gasmark concluded as he felt a wave of warmth engulf him, was the perfect icebreaker.

17

   Despite having a heavy heart, Sally had returned to her own flat that afternoon. Gasmark had felt some need in her to resolve her feelings and he let her leave early, reassuring her that he could cope solo for the last hour of the working day.

She needed space to put everything into perspective, and although she knew Rock was going to be there, another evenings silence wouldn't be anything new. It might even reinforce her thoughts and make what she had to do in the coming days easier to execute.

But as it happened, once the key had been turned in the lock and Sally had entered, she did so to emptiness and silence. Rock was not in the flat, and not squirrelled away up in the attic either with his blueprints and inventions.

Letting out a long sigh, she swung her bag onto the armchair and moved into the kitchen to put the kettle on. Although she had only spent one impromptu night away, the flat felt different and alien and cold. Almost as if she didn't belong there anymore. She shook the thought from her as she reached into the fridge for the milk. The sudden chill from the open door brought the sensation of alienation back and she cursed herself for being so touchy.

The click of the kettle coming to the boil diverted her thoughts and she busied herself with tea bag and milk before one final squeeze and dropping the spent pyramid into the bin.

Holding the mug she walked through the lounge and down the short corridor to the bedroom. Poking the door open with her foot the bed seemed to take up more of the room than usual, but Sally felt it mocking her. It no longer offered comfort. It was somehow as if it, too, had done the maths and knew of her infidelity.

Turning back she returned to the lounge and flicked on the stereo, not caring what music filled the silence, as long as it filled the silence.

Because, sipping her tea, it felt like the very emptiness of the flat was an accusation of her actions and it bore down on her with surprising weight.

Was this guilt? She wondered.

She tried sitting, but felt the need to move around; but when she got to her feet and walked about it only reinforced that she wasn't comfortable in her own home...because it no longer *felt* like her home.

Eventually she managed to settle and was sat on the sofa, reading her book, chin resting on her pulled up knees when Rock arrived home. He took the gull-head of his costume and hung it on a hook behind the front door.

"Hi honey, I'm home," he said sarcastically and, Sally thought, with a touch of spite.

Without waiting for a response he waddled through into the kitchen and it was then, as he passed by her, she noticed he was carrying fish and chips. For a moment she felt her cheeks flush with guilt.

It wasn't fish.

Rock reappeared from the kitchen having taken off the outer wrapping. Popping a chip into his mouth he sat at the other end of the sofa and extended the food, "Seagull?"

Sally concentrated on her book, feeling Rock's accusing eyes on her.

He had been to the van. He had spoken to Gasmark. He knew. But how? Gasmark wouldn't have said anything, of that she was sure. She thought.

"Not just now," she said trying to hide her irritation and multitude of other feelings that were clamouring for a space to be heard, "I'm trying to finish this chapter."

"Suit yourself," Rock said and leant across to the coffee table to pick up the remote. And there he sat, eating the very foodstuff that she'd been serving to customers all day with her new lover. Making satisfied noises each time he took a mouthful that, to her ears, sounded like a mockery of lovemaking.

The channels skipped from one to the other as he surfed for something of interest. Or perhaps to underline something unsaid. A snatch of a soap, a few seconds of a gardening programme, a minute of a reality programme involving celebrities.

Try as she might to ignore him and his constant, dissatisfied stabbing of the remote control and concentrate on her book, the more she found she was becoming worked up and annoyed. She could feel it building inside her, bubbling and spitting its way to the surface.

Soap.
Gardening.
Quiz.
Reality Celebrities.
Soap.
Quiz.
Gardening again.
Soap for the third time.
More Reality Celebrities.

Until she could take it no more and slapped the book shut.

"Rock...do you have to?"

He ignored her and switched channels again. This time to a local news report. A reporter was standing by the Quay holding a microphone and looking earnestly into camera as she delivered her report to the studio.

"...Where the town's population of seagulls has dropped dramatically."

Sally looked up, suddenly interested as the reporter continued: "A spokesman for the Council said today's figures vindicated the current policy of feeding..." before the screen jumped back to five traveller bridesmaids trying to squeeze into mandarin-coloured dresses with twelve foot trains.Sally nearly leapt from the sofa.

"No no no no... Put it back on!"

"It's only the news."

But she was adamant, "Put it on, put it on," and in her frustration leant across and wrestled the remote from Rock's hands and switched it back to the news report, "Feeding what? What are they feeding them?" she demanded, but the reporter has gone, replaced by a studio presenter moving onto the next item.

"Oooooh!" she shrieked, and threw the control back onto the sofa in frustration.

Rock was impassive.

"If you're hungry, have some of this," he said, once more extending the polystyrene tray inside the paper. It was too much. She snatched it off him and hurled it across the lounge.

"How many more times, Rock," she yelled at her costumed boyfriend: "I don't want a bloody seagull!" reached for her bag and swept out of the flat, slamming the front door. The sudden jolt knocked the gull-head off its hook and it rolled on the floor, its sightless eyes gazing up at the ceiling and a its beak slightly bent from where it had landed.

As silence once again fell, Rock leaned forward and stabbed his plastic fork into a chip that had escaped Sally's wrath and landed on the coffee table and popped it in his mouth.

18

Sally didn't know where she was going. She didn't want to go straight back to Gasmark's. Turning up in this sort of mood, which would only lead to a flood of frustrated tears was no basis for a new relationship. If she walked into his life she wanted to do it with a clear head, not fogged by baggage and anger.

So instead she cycled. Sometimes fast and angry, sometimes freewheeling, sometimes weaving in and out of bollards, up wide avenues, down thin cobbled streets, across pedestrianized areas, overtaking the three mobility buggies that snaked through the town in convoy at the strangest of times until finally she found herself freewheeling along the Lower Coastal path towards a line of the brightly coloured beach huts.

Up ahead in the gathering dusk she saw a familiar figure at turns staggering and tottering unsteadily on his feet. Clearly the worse for drink he toppled over onto the ground.

Approaching, she swung her leg over the crossbar and hopped off the bike while still steering it. Bringing it to a stop she let it fall to the ground and ran the short distance to help the familiar drunk to his feet.

"Horry?"

The usually amiable and friendly itinerant reeked of cheap alcohol and his voice was thick and hoarse, "Bugger off!"

"Horry? It's me...Sally. From Gasmark's burger van."

Horry accepted the support at his elbow and pulled himself to his feet. There he swayed, leaning towards Sally, fixing her with his rolling eyes until she stopped being multiple images and came into single focus.

"Ah," he said, "It's you."

Horry's situation was more than provident for Sally for it gave her something immediate and real to deal with and kept her from mulling over the situation she had left behind in the flat.

Her flare up hadn't been about Rock's idle flicking through of TV channels and she knew it. What niggled her was his choice words or emphasized phrases that suggested that he already knew of her night with Gasmark. But how could he? Unless he'd been following her.

And just why had he turned up at the van after she had gone that afternoon? It was almost as if he *were* following her, keeping tabs. The thought made her uneasy. It suggested the actions of an unstable mind, and in her book unstable also meant unpredictable.

"Where are you heading?" she asked, concerned.

Horry swayed, "Home," he said, indicating with a drunken flourish of his hand to the line of beach huts. In so doing he lost his balance, and would have fallen to the floor if Sally hadn't been there to catch him.

"Ooh, easy tiger. Isn't it a bit early to be this drunk?"

Horry's logic was plain: "Never too early if ya don't have a watch."

"And you live here?" All of the colourful huts were securely locked. They appeared well tended, and had been lovingly painted a variety of loud, livid colours. Looking down the line of them was like looking at a rainbow up close. A rainbow made of wood. In contrast to this sweep of colour, there was a lonely hut at the end that wasn't as lustrous in its paintwork. There was no evident padlock on its door and the felted covering over the roof was peeling and split.

"My castle," Horry slurred bouncing slightly as if his knees were made of rubber.

*

Lexxie had been walking towards the flat when she'd seen Sally rush off on her bike and had instinctively ducked back into the shadow of an overhanging wall as she sped past with the look of thunder on her face. She watched her go, as if making a decision.

And then she made it.

Walking on towards the front door of the building where she knew Rock lived; she rang the doorbell and waited.

It didn't occur to her as she was waiting for the door to be opened that Rock might not answer given the obvious circumstances of Sally's hasty leave-taking. As she saw it here was an opportunity for comfort and solace with the chance of making a step closer to getting Rock in bed.

The minutes dragged, and she rang the bell again before retracing her steps down the wide steps and stepping back onto the pavement. She peered up at the second floor of the tired looking Victorian building as she heard a sash window being pulled up. Sure enough Rock's head and shoulders appeared looking as if her were about to shout something and then stopped on seeing who was below.

"Rock?" she shouted up, "it's me. You busy?" There wasn't even a moments' pause. "Stay there!" he said, pulled his head back in and shut the window with an earnest *Ssssh*.

The view across the town took her breath away. She had never seen Folkestone from such a beautiful vantage point. The shore and the sea below, the horizon and the thin dark stretch of land across the Channel broken up by the very occasional and faint twinkle of light like a star that had fallen to the ground and was blinking for help.

Lexxie was standing on the flat area below the pitched roof, surrounded by a small wall. The open hatch beside her led down into the attic. As she soaked up the view she heard Rock returning up the ladder and presently his head poked out of the hatch. He was carrying a bottle of Shiraz and two glasses, but to her slight disappointment hadn't rid himself of the seagull costume that leant the scene a slightly ridiculous air.

"This is a great view," she said.

"And on a clear day you can see right across to France," he explained, filling a glass and handing it to her.

"I've been marveling at the twinkles of light over there. You come up here often?"

"Sometimes. Mostly after a row these days. It depends. Being this high up puts things into perspective."

"Where you up here were when I rang the bell? It's okay I saw Sally leave. Didn't look happy."

Rock said nothing as he poured himself a glass and Lexxie knew better than to push, especially when she had an altogether different agenda in mind. She sat and intentionally moved closer to him.

"Does she ever come up here?"

Rock shook his head. "She used to. Occasionally. She's scared of heights but won't admit it."

"What's the deal with you two?"

"What do you mean?"

"You're together but I don't get the feeling that you're together, if you follow me."

Rock shrugged, "I don't know. It doesn't feel alive right now. It feels...sort of paralyzed."

Lexxie leant forward and placed her wine on the ground before looking up and sideways at him with what she hoped was a degree of coquettishness. Her short, spiked hair giving her more of an air of Peter Pan youthfulness

"If you want my opinion, I think you're heading for a crash landing. Down in flames. No survivors."

There was a dropping of his shoulders, as if something heavy had just lifted. Clearly no one, least of all himself, had voiced this possibility.

"You think?" he asked. She nodded and placed a hand above his left knee and squeezed it lightly.

"We used to have fun, share the same sense of adventure, always up to something. Like we do. But all I ever get these days is nag nag nag about this job or that job. Life's not just about the material things, is it? It's about dreams and flights of fancy. That's where the real freedom is."

He paused, breathless. He realized that he had been wanting to say this for so long that the sudden release had taken him by surprise. "You ever read Jonathan Livingston Seagull?"

"Sure..."

"Remember the gull who sees farthest?"

"...is the gull who flies highest!" she smiled.

And it was there, at that moment, Lexxie knew she had bagged her bird.

Rock got to his feet, stretched his arms out wide and twisted round and round, imitating a gulls' flying and swooping.

"I'm that seagull and she's just stuck on the ground. Head in the sand. But me..." he climbed onto the small balustrade of a wall where his sudden exuberance had momentarily thrown his balance and he wobbled precariously for a moment before his centre of balance settled.

"Rock! Don't!" Lexxie cried out and leapt to her feet to save what she thought was a pre-emptive jump. Balancing better now, with his feathered arms perfectly perpendicular to his body, he calmed her.

"It's okay, I can fly. I'm a seagull and I can fly!" before letting out a squawk.

Lexxie laughed, realizing she had over-reacted and this was just part of Rock's horseplay.

"You're one crazy birdman, d'you know that?"

19

"Every time I think I should talk to him about the 'us' thing, he just seems to be either running around after another seagull or in his own world with those stupid inventions. It's pathetic. I can't talk to a man who's playing with a model aeroplane."

Sally returned to the customer and handed him his change.

"One fifty. Sauce is at the end there," and then turned back to Gasmark who had just lowered the next batch of freshly battered gulls into the spitting fat. "What are we going to do about him?"

For his part he was all in favour of the path of least resistance. Cutting off a blood supply like a clip on an umbilical chord and let nature do the rest.

"How about we say nothing and hope he gets the message that it's over?"

Sally put her hands on her hips, "What sort of advice is that? Jesus, are you men all the same?" Another customer moved to the front of the swelling queue as Sally looked at him, "Leg or breast?"

He looked back at her, pupils unnaturally dilated, and a line of saliva threading its way over the central crease of his bottom lip and onto his T-Shirt.

"Both," he said and placed a ten-pound note

on the counter. Sally looked at him harder and if she didn't know better she would have said he was stoned. Then, looking out at the crowd that had gathered, she thought that she could say the same about most of them. Something didn't feel right among the gathered throng. The way they seemed to sway as they waited. The lack of chatter that usually accompanied customers waiting in line gave the whole area a deathly quality.

She shivered at the thought of them all being fast-food zombies and returned her attention to the dribbling customer as she placed a leg and a portion of breast on the white tray and wrapped it in white paper. Taking one look at the fillets left she said, "Get some more birds done, we're running low."

Gasmark was already kneeling down looking through the fridge that seemed worryingly empty.

"Did you stock up this morning, Sal?"

"Yeah, while you were loading up a new gas cylinder. Why?"

He picked up a tub of margarine and waved it at her, "Apart from this, the cupboard's bare. Elvis has left the building."

"What?"

Gasmark stood up. "We're out of birds. Zippo. Zilch. Rien."

"We can't be, we had loads."

"Not any more. Look," and he stood back from the fridge.

Sally held up her hand to the next slavering, disconnected customer. "Hold on a minute," before squatting down to check the fridge.

It was empty.

Standing slowly she cast a look at Gasmark and then at the drones massing outside the van.

"Is there a problem?" someone said from near the front with just a tinge of panic in his voice. Like a junkie realizing their supplier may just let them down at the moment they need the hit the most.

Gasmark kept his voice low.

"What are we going to do?"

Sally could only think of one thing.

"Give us your phone."

The light coming through the stained glass windows of the church were radiant making the images depicted on the triptych seem alive. They certainly looked good through Nev's viewfinder as he slowly panned the camera round to come to rest on the highly polished Rosewood coffin that sat on a raised dais in front of the alter. He smiled to himself with the satisfaction of an artist as the light danced over the brass handles and name plate causing a momentary lens flare that only added to the beauty of the shot.

The mourners, all dressed suitably and traditionally in black - for there was nothing modern about this service - were all gathered, heads bowed as the Vicar held forth in the pulpit. This was the second time Nev had chosen to pan, and was hoping that the vicar wouldn't go on much longer as he was running out of ways to make the shot interesting. Too much panning and tilting would make viewers seasick.

"...And in our passing," the man of the cloth intoned with just enough of a singsong in his voice to keep the congregation interested, "we embrace the solemn tranquility often denied us in life. In our rest the eternal peace can never be broken by..."

The jaunty trill of a mobile phone ring tone broke the peace of the church. The air of collective grief was quickly littered with sharp intakes of breath and some generous tut-tutting of inconsideration. Nev himself cursed the interruption, as it would be difficult to edit out, until he realized there was a buzzing in his pocket that was in concert with the ringing. Sheepishly he brought his hand down to his pocket and pulled out his phone. He was just about to answer it when he chanced upon the disapproving gaze of the vicar bearing down on him from the pulpit.

Slowly he shook his head as if in question. The vicar shook his head in firm reply. Turning the phone off, Nev slipped it back into his pocket and returned his attention to the viewfinder.

"Sorry," he mouthed and then with more confidence than he actually felt said: "Okay, from the top again vicar, and ACTION!"

Having got no answer, Sally stabbed at the

phone in her hand, cutting the call.

"We're just going to have to tell 'em we've run out."

Gasmark looked uneasy.

"But it's not going to be easy. Have you seen the look in their eyes? It's like *The Walking Dead*. These guys have got the munchies something bad."

As if on cue, the van rocked violently to one side knocking Sally into him. At the same time, a wave of panic seemed to wash over the crowd like a tsunami as if they knew what was coming next. One customer nearest the front lunged over the counter. Instinctively Sally pushed him back.

"What're you doing?" someone close by asked as she reached out and attempted to pull the counter up.

"Half-day closing," she said hooking it to the top of the hatch.
Hands slapped the side of the van. A lone voice asked desperately, "Where's my Poulet?"

"All gone," she said by way of explanation, and then to Gasmark she urged, "Get the generator."

Outside the mood was beginning to turn as the news that the van was shutting up spread among the crowd of expectant customers.

"What's happening?" someone towards he back of the crowd asked plaintively.

"They're taking off!" said another as Sally quickly closed the flap and ran the bolts across, as the crowd surged forward and rocked the van once more.

Sally yelped involuntarily as she was thrown to the floor and Gasmark managed to drag the suitcase-sized generator inside and close the side door just in time. The rocked van slung Gasmark forwards and he landed on top of Sally who was struggling to sit up.

Disentangling them Gasmark pulled himself to his knees and clambered through to the driver's seat and slipped down into the drivers' seat.

"Hold on!" he shouted into the rear as she turned the keys in the ignition and gunned the engine.

Sally grabbed onto the work surface as the van lurched away. A customer grabbed at the windscreen as the van attempted a turn amongst the crowd of people and held onto a wiper momentarily before losing his grip and sliding off. Gasmark fought with the wheel to straighten up and, seeing an opening, drove ahead with grim determination.

The zombie-like mob couldn't bring themselves to accept the van was leaving, such was their addiction. This wasn't just a case of disappointment, this ran deeper and caused some to risk their lives and lunge at the van as it passed. Finding no finger holds they soon fell away like scales off a fish.

Looking in the wing mirror he watched the customers becoming smaller as the van made headway.

Turning onto the road he had to slam on the breaks as the convoy of three mobility buggies trundled by just as Sally was climbing through to the passenger seat.

The sudden jolt shot her headfirst into the footwell.

Throwing the van into first and continuing the journey Gasmark shot a quick look at Sally disentangling herself and coming to rest in the seating position beside him.

"I know you said you were a good cook," she said, "but this is ridiculous."

20

The first thing they had to do in order to avoid another situation that had befallen them this afternoon was stock up with more birds.

Nev had reluctantly agreed, complaining that it ate into valuable editing time, but was placated by the promise of a free pint once they'd finished and Sally had announced that she, rather than Rock, would don the seagull.

And so they met up shortly after the sun had gone down feeling like The Few.

That isn't what Fowler would have called them as he sat in front of the CCTV screens again stalking his prey. But whatever name he chose he was getting ready to call them to captivity. He let the proceedings unfold from the comfort of his chair. They needed to be under way before he gave the word to arrest them. There would be nothing gained from bringing in three individuals in fancy dress. He needed evidence. He needed dead gulls and video proof that they had been responsible.

And so he watched as the Seagull, Penguin and Octopus skittered about like 'Sealife On Ice'. All that was missing he mused was a pantomime horse. Again the traps snapped gleefully, and bags were filled, and yet again the security guard monitoring the screens alongside Fowler laughed at the very things he sneered at. He flicked the switch of the walkie-talkie in his lap.

"Stand by," he breathed over the static and waited patiently for the replies from his team lying in wait at strategic points around the beach. He sat back in his chair confident that this night would see a change in his fortunes. His dogged persistence, his compulsive studying of patterns of behaviour would come home to roost and he would be lauded. Watching the screens he stared at the ridiculous images playing out before him as if to challenge them to make a monkey of him this time.

The fact that he'd received an anonymous tip-off also helped.

As the night wore on Fowler began to stiffen for the final step and as he watched the two birds and cephalopod mollusk exchange a group 'high five' he knew his moment has come. With a grin he liked to think of as victorious he shouted into the walkie-talkie: "Go! Go! Go!" with such unexpected volume that Clive the security guard was taken aback and almost fell of his chair.

Satisfied that he had now set in motion the act that would bag him his quarry, Fowler got to his feet. "Oh yes," he said almost to himself, "oh yes. Got you now," and spoke again into the walkie-talkie: "I'm coming down," and left the room.

Clive watched the door close behind him and shook his head hoping to hell that Fowler was successful in his endeavour so that he wouldn't have to endure another night with him peering over his shoulder like a hawk.

Somehow, being dressed as an octopus and giving a seagull a kiss didn't feel at all strange to Gasmark. As long as the seagull in question was Sally.

As they pulled back from each other he noticed that her cheeks were flushed with the evenings' enterprise. Or perhaps, he allowed himself to think, it was the kiss, when suddenly an authoritarian voice from the shadows said,

"Excuse me, gentlemen... Can we have a word?" and a group of black-clad men and women with *SPG (Seagull Prevention Group)* embroidered on their tunics and police officers carrying nets, emerged from the dark of the shadows.

Nev's eyes widened.

"Shit! Run for it!" he yelled and lobbed his bag of seagulls up into the air and ran, prompting Sally and Gasmark to do the same.

Amidst the melee, not made any easier with dead seagulls raining down on them, Gasmark took hold of Sally and pulled her away. But there seemed to be more shadows disentangling themselves from dark recesses of buildings and boats and they only managed to move a few hurried steps in one direction before having to stop and choose another.

In the confusion, as he tripped over one of his tentacles, Gasmark stumbled to the floor and let go of Sally's arm. By the time he had righted himself and looked up, she had gone and sensing an incoming net he ducked and rolled out of its way, causing two policemen to rush headlong into each other and entangle themselves in netting instead of him.

Half running, half stumbling down a small slip way that led to the harbour, Gasmark thought he saw Sally running and flapping her wings at same time being pursued by one of the shadows.

Nev, careering round a corner in his flight, ran straight into a couple of unsuspecting members of the *Seagull Protection Group* knocking them all to the ground, and by the time he'd managed to wriggle free realized he was staring right at a pair of size twelves belonging to a Police Constable who had arrived on the scene.

"Long way from home aren't we?" the owner of the shoes said with the flat tone that passed for sardonic wit amongst the force. "Come on, up you get."

Sally's journey to the waiting police van was less dignified, and it took three officers to carry her, flapping and kicking and screaming. But their end destination in both cases was the same.

It was only Gasmark who escaped the clutches of the law after accidentally falling into the harbour as he'd fled from his pursuers who, not seeing what had happened, thought he'd just out run them.

"Too many legs, Sarge," he'd explained into his handset, "I didn't stand a chance."

By the time he'd judged it safe to pull himself sopping out of the sea and climb over the wall everything in his part of the harbour had gone quiet, and he watched as the police van moved slowly away.

For a while he sat dripping in the dark, trying to get his breath back and pulling strands of seaweed from his costume. It was only when he heard people approaching that he decided he should make a move, and he squelched away into the night.

*

In his attempt to avoid being seen by anyone, Gasmark took a circuitous route home avoiding streetlights. By the time he had reached the zigzag path leading up to the Leas Cliff he had taken to practicing his French verbs out loud to take his mind off how cold and wet and wretched he actually felt:

"I walk... *Je marche.* You walk... *Vous marchez.* We walk... *Nous marchons.* They walk... *Ils marchent.*"

As he turned a corner, he stopped to wring out one of his tentacles and watched, satisfied, as a stream of water tricked onto the ground and began to snake its way down the path.

"I am wet... *Je suis mouillé,*" he observed.

"Well, ain't you the linguist?" a voice said.

Gasmark froze and turned to face the direction he believed the voice to have come from. Of all the revelations, he somehow didn't expect it to be Rock peeling himself out of the shadow like Harry Lime in *'The Third Man'*.

Sally had worn his seagull costume and Gasmark realised that this was the first time he'd seen Rock in ordinary clothes for ages.

"You were right," he observed circling the sopping octopus with a look of disdain, "you do look a prick in that get-up."

"Rock..." was all Gasmark could think of to say.

"I would say slippery when wet," he replied bitingly, "but you've been slippery for a while, haven't you?"

He knows, Gasmark realised and the knot in his stomach tightened. But Rock hadn't finished with his oblique threats.

"I see they got my message then? What happened? I thought you'd be at the station by now facing charges."

"You tipped them off? Why?"

Rock shrugged. "Public duty. Oh no, wait a minute, what's the word? Oh yeah, that's it: revenge!"

Gasmark looked at the cuckold and realised that, whether Sally liked it or not, this was the place their lives changed. Rock was clearly not finished. His anger was rising as he stopped circling Gasmark and faced him.

"I saw the both of you, down there in the Amphitheatre."

"You were spying on us?"

"I was out for a walk and wasn't expecting to see my GIRLFRIEND with her tongue down her employers' throat."

"Technically Lenny's her emp..." Gasmark began when he was silenced by a sudden unexpected lightning bolt of pain that exploded in the centre of his face and he staggered back against the handrail. Instinctively he brought his hand up to his nose and felt the warm, unmistakable stickiness of blood.

Rock was holding his fist in pain. Surprised that such a punch should have hurt him.

Gasmark went on the offensive. "Look, *Th*-al turned to me becau*th*-e she'*th th*-ick of feeling invi-*th*-ible and ignored," but realised his swelling nose made him sound like an idiot.

"So that makes it okay, to just large in like Casanova? I should've guessed really, she's never been able to resist a bird with a wing down."

"She'*th* been pretty depre-*th*-ed about the whole *th*-ituation for age-*th*, and you never noti*th*-ed."

"And the only way to cheer her up was a happy-shag, is that it?"

"You ba-*th*-tard," he said and attempted a swing at Rock himself forgetting he was still in costume and instead of landing a punch, all he managed to do was wet-slap him across the face with a wet tentacle.

Neither of them were natural pugilists and together they cut an absurd sight as they attempted to punch and grab and kick at each other. The fact that Gasmark was dressed as an octopus didn't help, and from a distance the fight, such as it was looked like it involved more than just two people.

Rock managed to get to his feet and was

gasping for air just as Gasmark lunged at him in a half-hearted rugby tackle which took the both of them back down onto the ground and then suddenly rolling helplessly down the incline accompanied by a mixture of grunts and pained yelps.

When they finally came to a stop, Rock had just enough strength left to get to his feet and splutter, "Oh, I forgot to give you this," and delivered a well aimed kick to the molluscs that left Gasmark choking for air that wouldn't come to his lungs.

"Merde," was all he managed as he watched Rock stagger off down the zigzag path before passing out.

21

If the night hadn't gone particularly well for Gasmark he could have taken some comfort from the fact that neither had it proved the out-and-out success Fowler was pinning his reputation on.

The two fancy-dressed culprits had been apprehended and taken to the police station but at no little cost to his own team. Derek Clancy had got himself tangled in his own net and while trying to disentangle himself had walked squarely into a lamp post and knocked himself out. Two more had been involved with a head-on collision with the penguin and had been taken to A&E with hairline fractures and suspected concussion.

But whatever the personal cost to his team, Fowler had taken pride in seeing two of the law-breakers herded into the back of the waiting police van.

"Where's the third?" he asked as a Police Constable closed the door, "Where's he octopus?" The Constable had shrugged.

"Done a runner. They're buggers to catch. It's the legs."

"The legs?" Fowler asked, looking at the Constable as if he had gone mad.

"Eight of 'em."

Things hadn't improved when he returned to

the station in the morning. For a start he hadn't been allowed to interview the suspects and then he began hearing worried talk of Amnesty International.

As the day wore on and the morning slipped in to early afternoon, any hopes of triumph were draining away faster than water through a net.

"What do you mean, you're letting them go?" he almost screamed at the Police Sergeant when finally told the news late in the afternoon. The policeman had brought in a mug of tea to soften the blow.

"It's simple enough, Mr. Fowler, there's not enough evidence to charge them." Fowler was beside himself. He'd planned last nights proceedings down to the minutest detail, put in the hours of surveillance, observing patterns in location and days only to be told by this wheezing jelly of a Desk Sergeant that they were letting the brace of prisoners out without charge.

"But they're guilty," he stated emphatically.

The Sergeant nodded in a manner he hoped translated to empathy. He understood Fowler's black-and-white view of the world. As a police officer he came across it more often than he liked to think was healthy, but above all he was a duty bound respecter of the law and the innocent-until-proven-guilty tenet. Furthermore he was also painfully aware that if they proceeded with the charges on what little concrete evidence they did have, any judge would throw it out and lodge an official complaint about police wasting time and money bringing such cases to court.

He pulled himself up to his full height in the hope that his official status would carry some weight.

"Guilty of what, precisely?" he asked, "Arsing about in fancy dress, or just wasting police time? Unless you can supply any hard and fast proof, we're going to have to let them go. The seagull's already started on about Human Rights. She'll be squawking for the RSPB next! I'm sorry, but there it is."

"What about those traps and all the seagulls they've been...stealing under the cover of night?"

The Sergeant looked at him straight, like only a policeman could, "No sign of them. And as for the traps...apart from nearly taking the finger off one of my Constables." he put his hands in his pockets and leaned back on his heels as if to draw a line under what he had just said.

Fowler was impotent with rage. He felt like he had just been gelded by the authorities and he stood clenching and unclenching his fists in barely contained rage. His face was red with fury, on the verge of launching a diatribe leveled at incompetencies within the force, but the dutiful civil servant who always did things by the book and was a great believer in conducting matters according to the rule book called from deep within him at this his darkest hour, and pulled him back from the edge.

He walked to the internal one-way window that connected this annexed office to the front desk and forced himself to think straight and logically and not react any further. Behind him the Desk Sergeant allowed a tiny smile to creep across his face and he shook his head.

As Fowler looked out, Nev and Sally were brought to the desk to be signed out. They couldn't see him but his eyes bore into them and his lips curled with untrammeled hatred. It was the girl who interested him more. Something about her face and confident countenance niggled him. He was sure he'd met her somewhere before, but couldn't put his finger on it.

"Where have I seen you?" he breathed, leaning so close to the window that his nose touched the glass and condensation clouded up a small area when he spoke.

As he waited for Sally to sign her name, Nev caught sight of the local paper lying on the desk and pulled it across to read. It was the headline that had piqued his interest: *"COUNCIL CLAIMS SEAGULL DRUG POLICY A SUCCESS"*.

He picked up the paper and skim-read the story, before slipping it under this wing as if he were a commuter waiting in line to buy a train ticket, and upon signing his own name, turned and waddled out with the seagull.

*

By the time he arrived at the Environmental Health & Licensing Office later that afternoon

Fowler had prepared himself from the barrage of humiliation and jokes aimed at his failure, but to his surprise the mood as he stepped through the doors was rather muted. There actually seemed to be work taking place at most of the desks, and the gentle tap-tap-tapping of fingers on keyboards replaced the usual increased noise level caused by post-adolescent ribaldry.

Even Ashley, feet up on his desk reading a paper, wasn't his usual jocose self. Looking over his newspaper he didn't even bother with a crass dig at the Seagull Prevention Group. Instead he simply said: "The police didn't charge your GM Terrorists then, I take it?"

Fowler shook his head and sat down in his chair at his desk. "The fools. Said there wasn't enough proof. I suppose I'm the laughing stock of the office once more. Fowler cocks it up again."

Ashley didn't rise to the bait. The perfect opportunity to wind him up and make yet another joke at his expense and he didn't take it, which made Fowler think that he must be sickening for something.

"You just need to lighten up," he said, "Don't take things so seriously."

"What I *need* is a break. Some clue as to what they're up to."

Ashley put his paper down and leant on the desk, "It's always the big conspiracy with you, isn't it?" before sitting back in his chair and tapping the paper he'd just been reading, "Here, isn't this one of yours?"

Fowler had no idea what he was talking about. "Mmmm?"

"Gasmark's Gourmet Goodies. Didn't you visit that recently?"

"I did. Yes. Why?"

"What's the food like?"

Fowler hunched his shoulders and blew out his cheeks.

"It's not going to win any prizes, if that's what you mean."

"Oh no?" he said, picking up the paper and reading from it, "Well, listen to this: *Forget nouvelle cuisine",* he says, *"a fast food 'Van-extraordinaire' on the Folkestone seafront is serving up a culinary treat in the shape of Euro Poulet..."*

"Let me see that," he said, reaching across the desk and taking the paper from Ashley.

A cog whirred and ticked in his brain; synapses sparked and jumped to make connections as his eyes ran over the words written, in glowing purple prose by Jacob Oasthouse - self-styled 'People's Prince' of food criticism renowned for his championing of small independent restaurants and obscure dishes - of his newest, surprising discovery on the very edge of the South coast.

Lenny sat in the corner of one of the pubs he had a generous interest in engrossed in a newspaper article that the landlord had shown him.

"...A sweet and addictive dish that elevates the senses to taste heaven. But don't take my word for it, follow the crowd and find out for yourself. *Gasmark's Gourmet Goodies* really deserves to be on the map."

He lowered the paper with the look of an oncoming storm etched into his features. "Does it indeed? I'll put the little shite on the map all right," he said, shaking and folding the paper in one swift, angry motion.

"Boys!" he shouted, and his two muscle-bound acolytes, Scotty and Bill turned from their places on the bar stools where they had been enjoying an early liquid lunch at the landlord's pleasure.

"Drink up, it's time tae kick some arse!" And finishing off his large Scotch in one mouthful, the bald, angry Scot got to his feet.

The newspaper with Oasthouse's glowing review of what Fowler considered to be a second-rate fast food burger van lay on his desk. The rest of the office had cleared for the day - a mixture of restaurant visits and flexi-time early departures leaving him alone with his thoughts. He sat in his chair facing the window with its view of the Channel. In the silence he sat, fingers knitted together mentally arranging and re-arranging the pieces of his puzzle. "GM Terrorists... French Chicken... Euro Poulet," he mused.

Like a bad dream with the needle stuck, he

kept spinning round on these three points, unable to make the next move. So he did what he had never ever done, and spun his chair.

Ironically it was this one out-of-character movement that gave him the next piece. As he spun round, his eye caught the headline, just as Nev's had done earlier at the police station, and although he had seen it before, and also been aware of the findings held within the report upon which the news story was based, it was not until this moment that it took on any particular relevance when it tagged itself onto his stuck record and suddenly the tune jumped.

A light came on and he made the connection. He suddenly realised the reports claim had got it wrong. Seagull numbers hadn't fallen because of the doping of the bird population with a new breeding suppressant, they had fallen because they'd been culled. Culled illegally and then sold on as food.

"GM Terrorists...Disappearing seagulls...French Chicken... Euro Poulet!" It was obvious. It had been staring him squarely in the face and he had been too wrapped up in the cleanliness of the spatulas or the ensuring the cooking oil got changed on a regular basis to realise what had been under his very nose on that first visit. No wonder he had never heard of Euro Poulet before, it didn't exist.

They weren't selling French Chicken, they were selling Seagulls. And drugged seagulls at that.   Fowler didn't know what specific chemicals had gone into the breeding suppressant pellets used in the trial, but he was sure they wouldn't be viewed on as fit for human consumption. But now, thanks to the irresponsible actions of some half-baked entrepreneurs, growing numbers of the public were ingesting them without even knowing it.

Finally Fowler had a mission. He stood and looked out of his window, rolling the newspaper up in his hands and then slapping it down into his open hand.

"That's who she is!" he said, finally putting the pieces of the jigsaw together to create the full picture; a picture in which the girl from the police station featured slap bang in the middle.

Well, they wouldn't get away scot-free this time. But he couldn't accuse them head on. He had to be crafty. He realized that he had to go outside the boundaries of the law to bring them to book.

"Slowly, slowly catchy monkey," she said to himself. If the law wouldn't bring them to justice then the law was an ass and he would have to do it himself. He would go undercover and accumulate all the evidence needed. Then and only then would he strike.

With grim determination he walked round to Ashley's side of the desk and pulled open his bottom drawer and lifted out the pest control tranquilizer gun that Ashley had been showing off not so long ago. Alongside the gun was a small box of tranquilizing darts laid out in short neat rows.

The gun felt heavy in his hand, but not uncomfortably so. Knowing he was alone he turned with it and aimed at the filing cabinet on the other side of the room and felt the satisfying *'click'* of the trigger.

Filled with a new sense of purpose he reached into the desk and picked out the box of tranquilizer darts.

All the time a plan was forming in his mind. A plan of revenge and vigilantism. He would no longer follow the rules and strict procedure; he would do what Ashley had told him. He would lighten up. He would do the unexpected. He would veer off the rails. For if that's what it took to get his man, then Fowler would do it. Because in this new world, Fowler always got his man. And woman.

22

Gasmark had struggled home in the early hours. After Rock's departure he had pulled himself up onto the nearest bench where he had promptly passed out again.

By the time he awoke a few hours later the light of a new day was beginning to strafe the sky. His nose was throbbing and his head felt like it had been cleaved open, but at least the bleeding had stopped. Slowly, with all the caution of a post-operative patient he pulled himself into a sitting position before getting unsteadily to his feet. His lower abdomen throbbed dully following Rock's well aimed leaving present between his legs, and the very act of walking was wrapped in a blanket of aches, pains and twinges.

His muscles warned him of impending bruises all over and the discomfort caused by his wet and clinging costume meant that he had probably caught pneumonia into the bargain.

But at last he reached home, and putting a grateful key into the lock he pushed the door open and entered. The flat was in fact a maisonette, the basement and ground floor levels belonging to a chain-smoking woman vegan who owned an Irish wolfhound and the first and second floors belonging to Nev. Quite where he had got the money to invest in property Gasmark wasn't sure. He assumed a relative had died and left him money in a will.

With the door shut, Gasmark climbed the staircase to the first floor and then rounded the banister to haul himself, exhausted, up the shallow stairs to the top floor and the bathroom where he proceeded to run a hot bath.

Peeling off the clammy octopus garb he threw it onto the floor where it sat, creating its own little pool of water. As the bath filled, Gasmark wiped the steam from the bathroom mirror on the wall and contemplated his injuries. His nose was the most visible damage but after tweaking it tenderly he didn't think it was broken. There were other cuts and bruises but nothing else that would cause long-term damage, merely short-term discomfort. Somehow, he thought to himself as he lowered his battered frame into the hot water, he felt better for the fight as it had wiped away that nagging feeling of guilt. His relationship with Sally was now in the open and whatever happened from here on in could only be a positive thing.

He slid below the surface and allowed himself the brief sensation of being totally separated from the world.

If his personal affairs were being cleansed, his professional woes were far from assuaged by the previous evenings disaster. The police clearly knew about their nocturnal activities that meant that any further collection of gulls from the beach and nesting areas of Folkestone was out of the question. If they were to re-stock in the future they would have to spread their net further afield. Sandgate was being so close to Folkestone as making no odds, but Hythe was a possibility as was Dymchurch further along the coast to the West.

The main problem was if the van could be linked to the surreptitious gathering of seagulls. If it could, then he was sunk. He was certain that Sally, ever the thinker on her feet, would concoct some likely story explaining away their actions and be winging her way home at this very moment. And without any real proof of their real motives what was there to pin on them?
The steam rose off the surface of the water and he lay watching it for a long while, letting his mind drift around the problem.

As he was in this state he was startled by the loud flapping of a mature herring gull landing without grace on the bathroom window sil and proceeded too scrape its beak on the glass.

Not for the first time Gasmark was surprised at their actual size. Because they flew, and were often spied aloft rather than on the ground, the common misconception was that they were no bigger than a pigeon, but that was clearly not the case. That's what had made them prime for cooking - the sheer amount of bird one could get and, properly divided up, the amount of separate pieces. Nev had been right about the profit margin in that respect. And perhaps that was where the loophole lay. If the authorities clamped down and really went about a purge of fast food vans then that's exactly what they would be looking for.

Birds.

But if he wasn't selling birds, but burgers again, he would be in the clear. The only problem was after such dizzying success with the Euro Poulet, he couldn't bring himself to throw away all that by returning to cooking flat, uninspired circles of unspecified meat that everyone always assumed was beef.

He slapped a steaming hot flannel over his face and rested his head on the end of the bath to sooth his swollen nose.

Unspecified meat.

Unspecified.

Meat.

What was Euro Poulet if not unspecified meat? What were they trying to do if not hoodwink their customers? They were selling seagulls in the guise of French Chicken with a fancy fictional name. So that's what the authorities led, he had no doubt, by that snooping Health Inspector would be looking for. Seagulls. Not burgers.

So Seagull Burgers would probably pass under their radar.

He sat up in the bath with such force that great handfuls of water sloshed over the side onto the floor.

It was such an obvious alternative that he was shocked that he hadn't thought of it before. Mince the birds and make burgers out of them.

And forget Euro Poulet. Just sell them as *Coastal Burgers*. Unspecified meat that wouldn't matter because the taste was delicious - that much had been proven.

He stood up in the bath and stepped out onto the floor, grabbing his towel from the rail and proceeded to dry himself as fast as he could.

By the time he had dried and pulled on a T-Shirt and a pair of shorts he had the recipe all laid out in his head, and was downstairs in the kitchen pulling the food processor out of the cupboard.

The plucked and filleted seagulls he still had in the fridge had all been taken out and washed and sat ready on he work surface alongside a small collection of herbs and spices he was going to use to complement the meat and conjure up a whole new variety of blended burgers: basil, cinnamon, dill, fennel, garlic, ginger, lemongrass, mustard, paprika, saffron, sage, tarragon and thyme.

If truth were told he couldn't answer why they hadn't gone down this route before. Perhaps it was because it all happened so fast from the moment Nev had arrived with the road kill to the first flush of success. They hadn't needed to think about turning the bird into a burger because it was already selling so quickly. They were veritably flying out of the fryer. This way, he also realized, a single bird would stretch even further. As far as he could see his bath-time epiphany was a win-win situation all round.

His mobile phone trilled loudly in the silence of the flat jolting Gasmark awake. The very movement sent lightning bolts radiating out across his body from the centres of acute pain. He had fallen asleep approaching three o'clock on the sofa and now, in his foggy confusion was groping around the floor for the phone that he finally found under the edge of the sofa.

"Hello?"

"Gasmark, where are you?" Sally's voiced woke him up completely.

"At home…where are *you*?"

"Just been kicked out of the police station. No charges. Just a caution to stop with the stupid pranks."

"Where are you going now, home or…?"

"I'm with Nev. We're coming home."

Gasmark smiled. He would remember that single simple sentence for a long time after even though' Sally often claimed that it was a slip of the tongue Gasmark knew otherwise.
We're coming home. She had made her choice.

"Are you going to tell me where you got that black eye or not?" Sally said as she stirred her coffee. Nev had seen the state of his flat mate and sensed a *'responsible adult conversation'* looming, and on that premise ducked out to have a long hot bath, taking the paper he'd picked up at the police station with him.

"I slipped on some seaweed making my getaway," he lied unconvincingly.

"And there was me thinking you got it in a fight."

Gasmark looked at her suspiciously. She knew – he thought, and still she had come to him. Not Rock. "He told you?"

Sally's shock told him that he had just spilled all his cards. Damn!

"You had a fight with Rock? Oh my God! When?"

"He sort of...we, uh..." What to tell, what to leave out and more importantly what to embellish to guarantee a kiss from those beautiful half open lips.

"He knows...about us."

"And he hit you? Gasmark..." she got to her feet and came round to his side of the kitchen table, knelt beside him and laid a palm on his cheek. He flinched. Not because anything hurt, but just in case it was going to. "I hope you hit him back?"

"Well, we locked horns. I'm not sure it would qualify as an all out fight. It certainly wasn't the Thriller in Manilla."

"No-one's ever fought over me before", she said reaching up and kissing him on his lips, "My hero!"

"There's something else," Gasmark said looking into the swirls of his own coffee. Sally looked at him.

"He shopped us to the police. That's why they were waiting for us." For a moment she did nothing, but then got to her feet and, carrying the mug of coffee walked to the sink and stared out at the back garden, and the Irish wolfhound lifting its leg up against the fence having been let out by its owner.

For a long while she said nothing, and Gasmark took it as a sign for him to leave her to her thoughts. It was, he had to admit, a pretty big bombshell he'd just detonated in the conversation. He got to his feet and took his coffee into the lounge where he sat at the end of the sofa and waited.

At the sink she felt in her pocket for an envelope that had been burning a hole for the last two days. Now, she was certain, was the time to talk about it. She took it out and turned it over and over in her hands.

"This arrived yesterday," she said turning only to find herself looking at an empty seat.
She walked into the lounge and stood at the door, holding the envelope.

"What's that," he said, completely misreading the sign, "*Dear John...?*"

Sally laughed, and found herself relieved to do so. "No, more like Miss McIntyre"
Gasmark's faced signalled confusion. He wasn't following.

"I applied for a job," she said.

"You're always applying for jobs."

"This one was with Euro-Train. A marketing job in Paris."

There was palpable relief from Gasmark and his whole body seemed to loosen. Immediately her heart went out to him a little further.

"Oh yeah", he said, still unsure where the conversation was heading, "Well?"

"It's a yes. I got it, I got the job." There, she had said the very words she had begun to think would never be spoken, and she felt elated.

Gasmark stood and came over to her, smiling now. "That's fantastic, Sal. *C'est bon*! What are you going to do...take it?"

Sally turned the ball of her foot in mock coyness and laughed, "Thought I might, now I've got the Rozzers on me tail! Why don't you come with me? New start, new life...lost in France?"

"It's a big step."

Sally waved the letter like it was the golden ticket. "Hurry, offer ends soon!"

Gasmark was taken aback by the complete three hundred and sixty the afternoon had suddenly taken, and reverted to what he did best. Prevaricate and build protective obstacles.

"There's a lot to consider. I mean, the van..." Sally was ready to parry.

"Sell it."

"And the stock..."

"Bin it. What did you say about your spiritual home? C'mon..." she implored just wanting him to take that leap, "...take a chance."

"And Rock?"

"I'll leave him."

The sudden determination in Sally shocked him. But still the flame of indecision flickered.

He turned and paced, then looked over at her again.

"Really?" he asked trying to read her face. She just nodded, "After what he's done he can go and take a running jump."

Gasmark looked at Sally. Her face was promising a whole new unpredictable future and all he had to do was take that one small step. Sally looked at Gasmark, silently urging him on, closer to the edge.

And then he jumped. "Okay. Let's do it!"

Without thinking of his bruises Sally threw her arms round him and swung round.

"Fantastique!" she cried before realising the pain she was causing him, and pulled away. "I'm going to tell him right now," she said and disappeared back into the kitchen to grab her coat before returning. "You'll be alright?"

Gasmark shrugged then winced again, "I'll be fine. They're just bruises."

"Right," she said, "I'll bring plasters!" before skipping down the stairs towards the front door.

As the door clicked shut silence flooded the flat again. Gasmark stood shell-shocked by what he had just agreed to do. Finally he was going to get to France.

23

"Houston," Nev announced from the doorway, wrapped in a shower robe with wet hair gently dripping onto his shoulders as he rubbed it with a towel, "we have a problem."

While Gasmark and Sally were downstairs adding more bricks and mortar to their relationship, Nev was in the bath reading the headline story from the local paper and, despite his current location, experiencing a sinking sensation.

What he had just read would seriously put a huge spanner in the works and probably end the days of massed queues and sky-high returns. He got out of the bath and heard the front door shut. Looking out of the bathroom window he saw Sally's jaunty step as she made it down the steps and onto the pavement.

"Don't tell me," Gasmark said, "there's no more hot water?"

Nev held up the paper and tapped the headline?

"The birds are sick."

This was something Gasmark hadn't considered.

"Bird flu?"

Nev shook his head, "Not that kind of sick. Doped."

"What, seagulls on speed? Don't be soft." Gasmark took the paper that Nev held out and started to read.

"Not speed," his flat mate summarized, "but some sterilizing agent that stops 'em breeding. It's part of the Council's seagull population control programme. You just don't know what they feed animals these days. It's a disgrace!"

The horrible truth was beginning to dawn.

"You mean we've been feeding people doped seagulls?"

Nev nodded, "Technically, yeah, but keep it in perspective they've been putting additives into food for years."

"There's a shed load of difference between a couple of E numbers and turning half the town into smack-heads, Nev."

"Basic supply and demand! That's all you need to worry about."

"It's the supply that's the problem! That and the authorities. If this keeps on the way it is, we're gonna fetch up in prison."

Gasmark walked towards Nev, slapping the newspaper against his chest as he walked past.

"Where are you going?"

"To empty the van. I'd made Seagull burgers earlier this morning and took them down to the van's icebox ready for tomorrow. Now we're gonna have to get rid of the lot before a customer dies, or OD's."

By the time Nev had dressed and walked down to where Gasmark had parked the van, there was a dustbin bag full of discarded burgers on the pavement and the sound of disinfectant spray from within. He poked his head in through the side door.

"Just look at is as a setback."

"Until we get caught and they throw the book at us. Last night we were lucky but when they catch up with us Lenny will be the least of my problems."

The screeching of a Jaguar's tyres and the sound of a door opening interrupted the conversation. Nev climbed into the van.

"But not just yet," he said.

Gasmark glanced through the window anxiously and saw Lenny striding from the car waving a broadsheet newspaper, as Scotty and Bill squeezed themselves out of the back seats.

"Hey, Gobshite! I wanna word with you!"

"Oh perfect. Here, catch," he said tossing the keys to Nev, "I think we may need to move quickly."

Nev caught the keys and climbed into the front of the cab just as Lenny arrived at the side door and pulled himself up into the van.

"A little birdy tells me you've been making more money than you've been owning up to."

"What do you mean, Lenny?"

Lenny took hold of Gasmark's T-Shirt and pulled down hard, bringing his head into contact with the counter.

"Don't mess with me, chef boy. Fancy food critics waxing lyrical about your food and stating the queues stretch round the block. Unless you're giving this shit away I make it that your profits are up...and that means your APR's just gone through the roof!"

For the second time in as many days Gasmark's nose bore the brunt and began to bleed and throb horribly.

"It'*th* a *th*-imple mi*th*-take," he slurred, "Hone*th*-t."

Just then the vans' engine burst into life at the turn of a key and it lurched forward as Nev, unused to driving a vehicle of this size, hung onto the steering wheel.

Lenny, who had stepped back after landing Gasmark's face on the counter was suddenly wrong-footed and fell backwards out of the van, landing on his equally unsuspecting Muscle-bound gorillas.

The van grazed a car in front as Nev fought with the heavy steering wheel and Gasmark winced as he heard the familiar tinkle of smashed glass.

It shunted backwards as Nev threw the van into reverse and then continued his battle with the wheel before returning to first gear and stepping on the accelerator. This time he cleared the parked cars but in his flight, the front bumper caught the wing of Lenny's Jaguar that had parked up in the road and tore a hole in at as it continued on in its wake.

Lenny, scrambling to his feet could not believe his eyes and most certainly not what befell his motor.

"My car!" he yelled furiously, running over to the stricken vehicle. The van coughed out an explosive cloud of smoke as Nev crunched his way through the gears and slewed round a corner and out of sight.

Meanwhile Lenny was apoplectic. "My car! Look what they've done to my fackin' car." Very soon the grief at having witnessed his precious car being carved up and the humiliation at having been summarily ejected from the van turned to fury and the need to save face. Above all he wanted to teach Gasmark a lesson he wouldn't forget, and so climbed back into his car with murder on his mind.

After she had left Gasmark, bound for her own flat and a showdown with Rock during which she fully intended to clear the closet of unsaid frustrations and home truths and make it abundantly clear that the tatters their relationship had been left in was all down to him and his failure to grasp the realities of this world, Sally changed her mind.

Rock knew what had happened between her and Gasmark; that much was evident. The fact that he had betrayed them to the authorities was also a clear indicator that whatever love or loyalty he might have had for her had evaporated. So what was the point in reiterating what he already knew? Would it, rather than giving her satisfactory closure on their relationship actually make Rock the cuckold. The martyr?

She stopped in her tracks and considered this.

Looking out at the sea she said: "You never lose sight of your dreams, not if you never take your eyes off the horizon," to no one in particular.

Horry's words fluttered about her like butterflies on the wind. He had been right, she had never stopped believing in her dream job, and now she had it. Instantly she knew that it was not Rock she should be heading towards, but Horry. She owed him a debt of thanks and a few cans of Special Brew at least. He always had an ear for her problems, and always managed to put the whole world into perspective at the same time.

Digging her hands in her pocket she turned and headed down towards the seafront and onto the Leas Coastal path that she now knew led to Horry's temporary abode. Given the time of day he would either be there or at the very least on his way.

As it transpired she didn't see him on her way and she arrived at the beach carrying her bag of gratitude and tapped on the slatted side of the hut.

"Horry? Horry, it's me, Sally," and waited for a reply, or the sound of movement, but none came. "I've got some news...and booze. Thought we could celebrate."

Stepping into the hut she was suddenly hit by a smell that was repulsive. She put her hand up to knee mouth and resisted the reflex to gag as the smell clawed at the back of her throat. In the corner, amidst the rubbish and filth and the empty beer cans, was something familiar.

Stepping further inside, she reached out a hand and immediately recoiled.

"Oh...no," she breathed, put both hands up to her mouth and dropped the cans which rolled out on the floor as the thin carrier bag burst open.

In the days to come Sally would say that the only reason she returned to her flat and not Gasmark's was that it was nearer, and that it was an emergency. Whatever it was that drove her to run home, the key rattled in the lock just long enough to turn the combination, and she was inside, hot and breathless but with a focus: to find the phone. Which was not sitting in the cradle where it should have been quietly charging.

Frantically she looked around for the simple plain white handset, which looked more like a bone than a telephone. It wasn't on the sofa, or the coffee table. Had not been placed on the bookshelves, or left in the kitchen. She picked up the cushions.

Nothing.

Under the furniture, nestling on the floor with the fluff.

Nada.

On top of the TV with the remote control.

Neiht.

The fear and panic and frustration were building inside her. She ran down the short corridor and into the bedroom where the duvet curled up in the middle of the mattress like a giant walnut whip. She picked up both ends and shook it.

No phone.

Neither was it on the bedside cabinets, under the pillows or on the floor.

The phone had disappeared.

It was then she gave a frustrated cry and threw the pillow she was holding at the wardrobe.

Gradually, as her feeling of helplessness threatened to take over and consume her usually calm and confident personality, she was aware of a dull hammering coming from upstairs. She looked towards the ceiling, determined and headed for the loft hatch, which had been closed.

The stillness of Rock's isolated world up here in the loft space that had once been a romantic refuge for them both was suddenly smashed as the trapdoor opened, the ladder pulled down and Sally's head and shoulders appeared through the gap.

Lit by a naked bulb, Rock was seated, gluing seagull feathers to gauze-like material stretched over a wooden frame.

"Rock?"

With his back turned towards her he made no attempt to move or acknowledge that he had heard her.

She clambered up the ladder until she was standing surrounded by discarded bin-liners and the odd errant feather floating in the air.

"Rock...have you got the phone up here?"

barely turn a corner let alone a virtual three sixty. Are you crazy?"

Gasmark hadn't seemed to hear him, "But indicate left," he advised as calmly as he could.

Nev slapped down the indicator and prepared his whole body for the lurch to the right round the roundabout that was almost upon them. Gasmark, already strapped in, held on to the side door ready for the roll.

"Now!" he yelled and felt the whole cab lurch momentarily to the left as it banked the roundabout and then just as quickly lurch back and round to the right.

The engine screamed.

Nev screamed.

Gasmark screamed.

The whole world seemed to the both of them to freeze and then continue in slow motion as the trees and cars and Tarmac all stretched into one liquorice-long blur. Nev pulled down hard right and kept on pulling while crunching down through the gears that hollered their objection.

Wheels spun. Rubber burned. And then almost as suddenly as it had started, the van had righted itself, the blur of their surroundings replaced by the identifiable view from the drivers' window of a suburban street and the two incumbents of the van stopped screaming.

Gasmark's face was ashen and he noticed that Nev's was too. For a second there was silence between them, it then Nev broke the ice. Adrenaline kicked in and he began shouting and laughing and punching the steering wheel. He wasn't quite sure how he'd done it, but he had managed to throw the large, unwieldy vehicle into an almost full U-turn and shake off their crazed pursuer into the bargain.

For his part, Lenny, sitting crazed behind the wheel of his beloved Jaguar and screaming obscenities as the van ahead veered this way and that had completely bought that feint to the left.
"Got yer now, you worm," he mocked as the indicator flickered on and off as the van careered at speed towards the roundabout.
Gasmark's bluff had worked a treat. Thinking that his quarry's blind adherence to the Highway Code had given him the edge, Lenny stepped on the accelerator and bore down on the van which he mistakenly thought was slowing down as it leaned to the left, only to realize much too late in his own manoeuvre that he'd bought a pup. He let forth a string of obscenities as the car flew off to the right with him helpless to alter its course.

*

Dressed in his seagull costume, Rock was on the roof. After Sally had stormed out he had returned in earnest to complete his second wing, and now, rather than let the adhesive on the final few feathers dry he had taken them both up onto the roof to once and for all show his ex-girlfriend that his constructions were far from toys.

He stuck his forefinger into his mouth and then held it aloft. There was a slight wind, but not enough to hamper his plans. A piece of dropped cloth help determine the direction with slightly more accuracy, and once he was happy that his flight from the roof would take him over open park land rather than more houses he stepped back and picked up the left wing.

The wooden frame was light and flexible, and the feathers glued onto a tight gauze cover helped to create the appearance of perfect replicas of Daedalus' ancient design.

Working methodically, he began to attach both levered wings onto the central body harness that he had built. It consisted of a rucksack frame that had been stripped of its material so that all that remained were the adjustable shoulder and torso straps.

Once the wings had been secured he picked up the harness and turned it over and round his body so that very soon his arms had passed through the shoulder straps and he was able to hitch the body frame up onto his back and tighten the straps over his shoulder. He then drew the two straps around his waist and fastened them tight before it was time for the wings. Slowly he slipped his left arm through the loops and stretched towards the handle that stuck out midway down the wing; then carefully he raised and dropped his arm to feel the drag.

It felt comfortable. He repeated this with his right arm and, with both arms outstretched, drew both wings carefully up and then brought them down again. Up…and down as if reminding himself of the movement. He then rotated both arms in a slow sweeping figure-of-eight, mentally picturing a youthful Leonardo da Vinci doing something similar in Florence.

Finally feeling confident that all his pre-flight checks had been carried out, Rock stepped up onto the balustrade and lifted his head high.

Ahead of him, in the fading light was the sky, a huge waiting canvas upon which to be drawn, and below him, far below was the street. Rock reached out his arms at either side resembling *The Angel of the North*. He then looked down to gauge, for the last time, his height.

The street was quiet.

Again he looked straight ahead wondering exactly what it was that Sally had wanted from her life with him; where the point in the road had come that had begun to divide them as she took a more capitalist route and he continued with his dream. As he thought of it, with the wind blowing around him, he realised that it no longer mattered. She had made her choice. But the real future was here. Now. On this roof. Staring out into the darkness where anything could happen.

With this in his mind he pushed himself off the roof and into the void.

For a glorious moment, his dream of flight became a beautiful reality…he swooped and then caught the wind and soared a little higher. His dream now no longer something that could be mocked. He had done what Daedalus had failed to do...he had conquered flight.

He laughed as he glided, but then faltered as all the grace and beauty of his flight suddenly deserted him and he found he was no longer flying but plummeting.

In the dark he pitched headlong towards the ground where the only thing he was aware of as his wings flailed helplessly about him, was a set of headlights making their way slowly down the street.

Lenny was not a happy man. Despite the fact that his expensive Jaguar had been mauled by an ugly rust-riddled hulk of a van, and that van had out-run him what was really eating him up was the fact that he had lost them.

For over an hour the car, with Scotty squeezed in the back and Bill next to him in the passenger seat, crawled the side streets of Folkestone. He was convinced the van would have been parked up and the two jokers who had led him a merry dance gone to ground, but there was just a chance they would make a mistake, creep out of an alley, try and slip away unnoticed and he wanted to be right there when they did.

Shadows played their usual game with the casual observer, and as the car cruised the streets in the gathering gloom its occupants saw their quarries behind wheelie bins, next to lampposts, ducked into alleyways and skulking by bus stops. And every time they rationalized what they had just seen, the darkness came together again and spread out elsewhere to plan another way to tease the frustrated pursuers.

Just then Scotty caught something on the breeze; a sound that didn't quite fit; that didn't belong out here in the dusk. He strained to hear, and to him it sounded like it was getting clearer and, more importantly, getting nearer.

"Anyone hear that?" he asked, leaning forward so that his head poked in between Lenny and Bill in the front of the car, "that sort of high pitched..."

Then they all heard it. Screaming.

Becoming louder and getting closer with every second. It was coming from above.

As one they all looked up through the windscreen into the darkness and realized a horrible truth. They were, quite simply, in the wrong place at the wrong time.

What they saw plummeting headlong towards them, a mass of feathers and screams was not a shadow.

It was Rock.

The last thing that crossed his mind as he crashed through the windscreen with a bone-crunching smash was how he really should have paid more attention to where Icarus went wrong. Of course what he really should have done was let the glue dry on his wings but, stung by Sally's final taunt, pride had come before a fall in rather impressive and tragic style.

25

Despite ringing the doorbell for a fifth time, she knew it was helpless. She knew they weren't in, and it was that knowledge as much as anything else that made Sally crumple to the floor in defeat.

So much had happened over the last twenty-four hours and she had not really had time to sit down and take it all in. And now, as she sat on the steps leading up to Gasmark's flat it all came crashing down and her shoulders shook as she choked with great sobs. Some out of exhaustion, some out of relief and some out of pure despair.

Her relationship with Rock was now at an end and after months of grinding indifference that release was liberating. Her feelings towards Gasmark were growing all the time, and having persuaded him to join her in France meant that they would start that journey together; but it was Horry that she really cried for.

Looking up at Gasmark's window, she stood and in a final act of desperation cried out,

"Gasmark?" But there came, as she knew there would, no answer. The flat was in darkness. All hope was gone. At her wits end she could think of nothing else to do but kick the door in frustration.

A little further up the street two lights swung slowly into the road and approached cautiously. They had been edging ever closer to home but by the most circuitous of routes. Gasmark didn't want to run into Lenny again this evening, and so their journey home took in the widest possible circle.

As the van approached, Gasmark saw someone kick the front door and his heart missed a beat. After all they'd done to out run and out fox him, Lenny had simply returned to the flat and waited.

"Kill the lights," he breathed.

"What is it?" Nev asked squinting into the gloom. The small yellow pools cast by the occasional street lights didn't offer much in the way of illumination, and he craned his neck over the steering wheel.

"It's Lenny," Gasmark said as the van almost came to a stop. Nev caught the silhouette as it turned.

"Wearing a long wig and a skirt?"

"What?" said Gasmark staring harder. "Wait a minute, is that Sal?"

Before Nev could answer Gasmark opened the passenger door and had jumped down into the street.

"Sal?" he said approaching at a half-run. She turned towards him, the streaks of tears hidden by the darkness.

"Oh Gasmark, thank God!" she managed before succumbing to more sobs and ran into his arms.

Nev drew up silently in the van and looked at Gasmark.

"What's going on?" he mouthed.

Gasmark looked back over Sally's shoulder and mouthed, "Don't know."

*

Nev, Sally and Gasmark stood speechless at the door to the beach hut. They were in somber mood as they looked in. There was a mass of empty beer cans, some crushed and a pile of dirty blankets. Amidst the mess lay Horry.

Unmoving.

Nev was the first to speak.

"You're sure he's...?"

Sally had regained some of her composure and despite her sense of loss at the knowledge that Horry had passed away, common sense was kicking in, and she was beginning to think of practicalities.

"Of course he's dead," she said, motioning with her right arm at the immobile body half shrouded in his makeshift bedding, "look at him!"

Gasmark was in unchartered territory. He had never seen a dead body before, and now that he had wasn't sure of the next move.

"Should we call the police or someone?" he suggested.

"So they can just shovel him up and dispose of him like he was rubbish?" Sally argued, "He was worth more than that. We can't just abandon him like that."

"So what do we do?"

In the time spent on the steps at Gasmark's

flat Sally had broached this question herself and given it plenty of thought. She recalled all her conversations with Horry, all those dreams of freedom and far off travel that he'd waxed lyrical about. About his days at sea in some unspecified role. Sally had wondered whether they were of highly romantic origin like Merchant Seaman across the Indian Ocean, or simply working on the cross-channel ferries. Whatever they were, she had come to a conclusion of what to do.

"I think we should give him the send-off he would have wanted," she said and bent to pick up the '*Sail the Seven Seas*' brochure lying crumpled on the floor.

"A cruise?" Gasmark asked, confused.

"A burial... at sea."

Nev appeared less than convinced, "Hardly appropriate, is it, seeing as he obviously had an aversion to water?" and received as sharp dig in the ribs by Gasmark to shut him up. This was no time for glib remarks.

"I don't know about this, Sal. Don't you need permission for something like that?"

"Sod people's permission," she said turning to him, "let's just do it! Get a boat and bloody do it. It's what he would have wanted."

There was an awkward silence broken only by the 'whump' and 'hisss' of the sea beating the shore before being sucked back out again.

Gasmark looked at the body of a man he'd known only in passing. A man who had willingly taken leftover food at the end of a working day 'to help out' as he put it in order to retain his pride. A man who now lay lifeless and wretched with no-one to look after him in his final journey.

"Okay," he said, coming to a decision, "if we're really going to do this, we better do it properly."

He nodded to one of the wooden boats that had been hauled up onto the shingle out of reach of the tide. "Nev, go and find us one of them boats. One with oars."

Nev looked at Gasmark and then at Sally in the gathering gloom and the air of grim determination that clung to Sally's body told him that it was futile arguing. He turned and made off in search of a boat.

As Nev scrunched off across the beach, Gasmark leant over and picked up the nearest blanket and shook it out. Sally was smiling. He knew they were doing the right thing.

What neither Nev, dispatched to find a seaworthy vessel among the boats on the beach, or Gasmark and Sally, readying a shroud in which to wrap around Horry's body noticed was the small dark shadow hunched up in the trees above the beach huts. Dressed in camouflaged army fatigues, Fowler sat immobile, watching the proceedings through binoculars. Slowly he pulled out a Dictaphone from his jacket and whispered into it.

"Twenty-two hundred hours. In position. Suspects using a beach hut on the seafront, possibly for storage. Will investigate further at the earliest opportunity."

He was happy with how events had turned out. His decision to 'go rogue' and catch those responsible for taking a wholly irresponsible (and highly illegal) approach to fast food was paying off. All the pieces of his jigsaw puzzle had come together and, holding them in his hand, he had decided not to present them all to the police, but to go out on a limb and catch them himself, an Environmental Health Lone Wolf. For too long had he been bound by the rules of his job, bound by procedure and protocol. For years he believed that this was the only way to maintain law and order and food hygiene, but now, sitting wrapped in the shadows on the edge of the law, he realised he'd been wrong. Fowler now felt alive, vital and in charge. He wasn't hiding behind a rulebook anymore. He was making the rules. He *was* the law.

Lifting up his binoculars he scanned the beach and caught Nev in his sights. One by one he was moving among the upturned rowing boats in what looked, to Fowler's newly enlightened imagination, like highly suspicious endeavours.

"What are you up to?" he asked in a low whisper. There seemed no reason to what he was doing, and the more Fowler watched, the more he began to believe that Nev was searching for a secreted package; but a secreted package of what he had no idea. What he was certain of though, was it absolutely, definitely and without a shadow of a doubt had something to do with their seedy little illegal enterprise.

With these thoughts in his head, he swung the binoculars back in time to see Gasmark and Sally hauling some of their stock out of the beach hut in what, from this distance, looked like a tarpaulin. Then the realisation hit him like a shot of electricity. They were smuggling the gulls out of the country! Probably to a larger boat waiting out at sea.

"Good God," he breathed as he made connections that weren't there. By stepping outside of the law he had stumbled upon quite the most bizarre smuggling ring on the south coast. He raked the binoculars back across the beach and caught Nev pulling a boat away from the others and down the steeped shingle towards the sea.

Once the boat had reached the water Nev looked back across the beach and lifted his hand to his mouth. With the thumb and middle finger he whistled shrilly across the short distance to where Sally and Gasmark were carrying their contraband away from the beach hut.

Fowler watched rapt as they struggled to bring the large package across to the boat and then, with Nev's help, manhandle it over the side before dropping to the ground, exhausted.

He put the binoculars down and reached into his jacket for a Twix. Pulling the wrapper open he mused on his next step. As a one-man army he wasn't going to achieve anything by rushing them now. All they really had to do was run away and all he would have would be a mountain of dead seagulls with no proof that it was evidence of a surreal smuggling ring. No, what he needed to do was bide his time. If their intentions were to row out to a larger boat waiting in the darkness then that would give him time to make a thorough search of the beach hut and their wretched van which stood parked a few feet away.

    His smile widened at this logical plan of action, and settled back to for them to make their move offshore.

26

Gasmark had only ever put to sea in a boating lake before, and was finding the oars heavy and unwieldy as he pulled against the flow of the tide. Nev, sitting beside him was also finding the exertion heavy going but neither dared slacken or complain in the face of Sally sitting opposite them with the look of proud determination etched on her face. She had discovered Horry.

She had made the decision to honour his last journey with dignity and now she sat looking out towards the open sea thinking about the friend she had lost.

For his part Gasmark bit on his lip has he heaved the oar back again, feeling the terrible strain and resistance put up by the water upon which they were sitting. He had no real idea how much headway they were making, or even if they were heading out in a straight line. Every time he looked across at Nev all he saw was similar pain of exertion etched across his face. His eyes were squeezed shut and he was clearly finding the whole thing as difficult as Gasmark was.

Eventually, having put their backs into it, and heaved in union on every stroke, the boat found itself far from shore and in calmer waters than the choppy waves closer to the beach. Having rowed continuously for so long Gasmark lifted his oar out of the water and breathed the salty air deep into his lungs. Nev followed suit, and leant forwards over the oar, coughing.

"Are we out far enough yet?" he asked across the boat. Sally, who had been silent throughout the whole journey, wrapped in her own memories of Horry, looked about her. The lights of Folkestone twinkled in the distance, but the landmarks were too far away to distinguish.

Maybe in the daylight it wouldn't seem far, but here and now at this time of night, with no illumination other than that of the half moon, it felt like they had rowed out into the middle of the Channel.

Gasmark held onto the side of the boat as it rocked to and fro in the swell. Now wasn't the time to tell Sally he was a weak swimmer. He grimaced as a wave hit the boat and rocked it even more and wondered whether 'weak swimmer' wasn't being too generous.

Trying desperately not to rock the boat any more than it already was, Gasmark got up and edged around the shrouded body so that he was ready to pick up Horry's feet. Nev did the same, maneuvering himself into a position where he could lift Horry's shoulders.

He looked at the sea all about him and back to the distant shore.

"This should be far enough out to prevent him washing back up on the beach," he said. Gasmark agreed, "So... here we are then. D'you want to say something Sal, y'know before we push..." he stopped himself, before beginning again, "commit his body to the sea?"

Now the time had come, Sally looked a little lost.

She pulled a thread of hair away from her face and said in a low, respectful voice, "I don't know what to say," she began, emotion rising in her throat, "except happy landings."

With a nod from Gasmark, they heaved Horry's shrouded body up onto the gunwale of the boat and over into the sea. With a large splash, the body disappeared under the waves. Gasmark watched the water close in around the shroud.

"With a good tide he'll probably get to France before we do," he said almost enviously.

"Well," said Nev, returning to his seat and picking up his oar, "we'd better be getting back before the owner turns up and finds her gone."

Suddenly he was drenched in a fountain of water and Horry shot up out of he water, pulling the shrouded blanket from round him and gasping for air.

"Help!" he managed before slipping back under the water amid flailing arms. Seconds passed before he shot up again, mouth opening and closing like a demented fish as he sought more air to fill his lungs, "Help!"

Sally scrambled across to the starboard side of the boat where the drowning man had just gone under.

"Horry!" she screamed, "Man overboard!" As he surfaced again and began thrashing around desperately for something to hold onto,

Gasmark and Sally reached out to grab the tramp's sodden form.

"Help!" he croaked again in between great gulps for air, "I c-can't swim!"

"It's alright," Gasmark shouted, pulling him back towards the boat, "we've got you."

With great effort they pulled Horry back onboard with much less dignity than they had previously dispatched him. He sat in the well of the boat dazed and soaked but yet by all miracles, alive.

Sally took off her jacket and wrapped it around his shoulders, "Horry, are you all right? We thought you were..."

"I could've drowned!" he pointed out in between coughs.

All three of the crew exchanged guilt ridden glances while Horry caught his breath. It was left to Nev to see the positive side of their horrendous error. "Lucky we were passing then, eh?" he said.

"C'mon, let's get you back on dry land and dried out," Sally said which was as much a prompt for Gasmark and Nev to get rowing again as anything else.

*

Fowler lowered his binoculars as the tiny boat slipped out onto the sea. By his calculations they would be gone at least an hour, probably two which left him plenty of time to conduct a thorough search of their storage facility and van.

Plenty of time to gather evidence and most

definitely plenty of time to marshal his troops so that by the time the boat arrived back there would be no repeat of the other night. Caught red handed with no room for wriggling out of a conviction.

Fowler would be vindicated, lauded and very probably promoted away from the childish behaviour of Ashley and his goons. It was ironic that it was Ashley who had unwittingly provided the final piece of the puzzle that had led to Fowler tracking down the van to this point. And something more than luck that had brought the van speeding past him as he headed out for another nights camouflaged reconnoiter of the town. It was almost as if they were mocking him. Well, let the mocking be on the other foot now.

He stopped, not sure whether mockery could be on the other foot, before dismissing it. It didn't matter. All that mattered was his triumph.

Carefully he made his way down the earthy slope that had been his hidden vantage point and moved silently past the van and towards the beach hut. Stopping to look around him, he realized that the Council hadn't extended its CCTV network this far down the line of beach huts and was clearly why this end of the line had been chosen to store their contraband. With no-one watching, they would have been able to go about their illicit business unobserved.

Leaving the shadows, he half-crouched, half-ran towards the beach hut which he could see from the door ajar, was still open. Checking that no one was watching him, he ducked inside.

As soon as he stepped into the cramped space he was hit by the stench of stale urine, vomit and very possibly fecal matter also, but he didn't stay long enough to find out. His stomach turned and forced him back out into the fresh clean night air where he proceeded to retch beside the hut.

Whatever had been stored inside had clearly gone off. Immediately he began considering what Environmental Health regulations might have been broken. It was a wonder the place wasn't crawling with rats.

As he stood bent over, and leaning on the side of the hut while he retched, Fowler was suddenly hit by a clump of earth that had been thrown from somewhere deep in the shadows.

"What the...?" he said, looking up just as another smaller clump of earth caught him squarely in the face.

Staggering back he realized that he must have under-estimated the level of cunning employed by his nemesis. This sudden attack was a sharp comeuppance for his hubris.

From out of the corner of his eye he sensed more than saw another clod of earth find flight, and he ducked just in time as a gang of teenagers, feral-like and hooded came charging out of the bushes hurling insults and abuse as well as soil

"Tosser! Waster! Scrounger! Scumbag!" they yelled swarming around him, and raining down blows with fists, sticks and boots. Unable to do anything else, he fell to the floor and instinctively protected himself by curling up into a foetal position, covering his head with his arms.

Somehow, amidst this sudden and unprovoked attack a scuffle broke out amongst his assailants and suddenly there was a window of opportunity for escape. Daring to look up he saw that the eye of the storm had shifted and two of the hooded creatures had turned on each other and were now rolling on the floor punching and kicking themselves and not him.

Taking his chance he scrambled to his feet and stumbled away. He had managed to get fifty yards before his attackers realized their victim was making a bid for freedom and yelped and hollered after him, but Fowler was not taking any chances in looking back. Ignoring the deep cut to his head and sundry bruises to the rest of his body, he just ran intent on putting as much distance between himself and the pack of youths trailing after him as was humanly possible.

If Horry had witnessed the attack he would have taken solace from the fact that the group of teenagers attacked anyone they came across, and not just him.

27

The scene outside Sally's flat was one of unexpected light and activity at this midnight hour. The road, from both ends had been cordoned off with yellow police tape that fluttered and bowed in the slight breeze. Further beyond the tape the emergency services were represented by the blue flashing lights of an ambulance, a fire engine and sundry police cars.

A small crowd had gathered earlier, at the time of the accident when the activity was at its heightbut now had thinned so that only the most curious remained.

The first ambulance had left as soon as Rock and Scotty had been cut free from the crumpled wreckage of the Jaguar, and the second, containing Lenny and Bill and a passer-by who had tripped on a protruding paving slab and broken their wrist was just nosing its way out as Gasmark pulled up with Sally, Nev and Horry in the van. Sally leant forward in the passenger seat to see down the road to where police were gathered around the crushed car.

"What's going on here?"

Nev, squashed in the middle, pointed at the wrecked car, "looks like someone's had a nasty smash," he said, "but what's that sticking out of the roof?"

This time all three craned to look. The windscreen had been completely caved in and there were sizeable dents in the roof and thebonnet. In amongst the metal and glass lengths of wood stuck out at awkward angles.

Strips of gauze and feathers caught the breeze and lifted; only to be brought back by the stapled ends attaching them to the ends of the frames. A few errant feathers had been torn from the material and danced in small directionless circles on the ground.

Sally watched speechless as a police constable walked over to the car and lifted the wooden frames from the wreckage. In the process a few more feathers detached themselves from the gauze and fluttered off into the night air. Her eyes widened at the realization.

"Oh my God," she said, putting a hand to her mouth, "it's Rock!"

Before anybody could say anything else, she had opened the door and jumped down from the van. Lifting the yellow police tape she ducked under and ran towards the van, but was stopped by two policemen.

From their seats in the van Nev and Gasmark witnessed the whole scene as if watching a silent film. Sally looked from one policeman to the other, and then threw up her hands in protest. In a feint, she tried to sidestep the two officers and make for the car, but was caught by the arm by the second policeman and pulled to the side. Meanwhile the first officer was talking into his Walkie-Talkie before turning to Sally and, with very precise gestures seemed to indicate something had fallen from the rooftops and collided with a car while traveling along the road. Gasmark looked across at Nev, "Whatever's happened, it ain't good," he said as Sally was escorted away from the car and back towards the yellow tape and the van.

*

The footsteps, with a slight comical squeak on the linoleum floor of the hospital corridor every second step announced the medics' approach so Sally heard the doctor before she saw her.

The three of them sat side by side like three little monkeys on chairs awaiting news when the sharp-faced doctor appeared from the direction of the side room where she had been assessing Rock's injuries.

"Ms. McIntyre?"

Sally automatically got to her feet. "Yes."

"Let me say from the start that we're not quite sure yet exactly what happened, but..."

"He jumped, didn't he?" Sally asked although it felt more like a statement of fact.

If the doctor was surprised she didn't show it. Instead she stuck to the clear facts.
"We can't say for definite, it's too early. The patient will be going up to X-Ray shortly to ascertain just what he has broken. Looks as if he was quite lucky. His fall was broken by a passing car. The occupants weren't so lucky. Multiple fractures, apart from the driver. Still, worse

things happen at sea. There's nothing you can do at the moment except wait."

The doctor's bleep trilled and she looked at the display.

"There is a drinks machine by the lift if you fancy taking risks, but I'm afraid it does taste like creosote."

"Thank you," Sally said as the doctor trotted off towards the nearest phone, the step-squeak, step-squeak retreating at a quicker pace than it had arrived.

Gasmark looked up at the signs suspended from the ceiling telling them the direction of the lift.

"Well," he said glumly, "creosote it is then," and headed off down the corridor in search of the drinks machine, leaving Sally and Nev alone.

"You serious about Rock jumping?" he asked as Gasmark turned the corner and disappeared out of sight. Sally nodded.

"You don't think it was down to all those seagulls he ate?" he asked, "Turned his head?"

"What '*you are what you eat*'?" she asked rhetorically, "No, he was odd before that. I used to think it was sweet. Now I just think it's sad. A little boy hiding from responsibility in a fantasy world."

Nev opened his mouth to say something, but realized he had nothing of any merit to say about the situation. It was a rum state of affairs. He had been dumped himself many times in the past but had never once resorted to leaping off a roof in despair dressed as a bird.

A frail woman in fluffy slippers, an ill-fitting nightie and a thin toweling dressing gown was struggling with the drinks machine. She already had two drinks and the machine was busy attempting to dispense a third with a short series of coughs, splutters and unappetizing wheezes as Gasmark approached. She caught his eye and said balefully, "If you're not sick before you come in, this stuff'll make sure you are before you leave."

Feeling there was no suitable response, Gasmark simply said"Oh," and looked around to see a toilet door. He decided to go and freshen up after the nights exertions, figuring by the time he'd splashed water over his face and swilled some cold water round his mouth the woman would have taken her drinks and moved off.

Rather shockingly Gasmark thought for a split second that someone else was looking at him from beyond the mirror. His eyes were ringed red and the lines beneath the eyes were a sorry testament to recent events. He leant on the basin and peered closer at the face staring back at him. It had seemingly aged years in the few short hours since he had last looked in a mirror after his fight with Rock on the zigzag path leading up from the beach. The bridge of his nose was turning a nasty shade of purple and mustard yellow. The white of his eyes were veined and red and he had at least a couple of days' stubble across his chin.

He rubbed his hands through his hair, scratching his scalp and wondered whether he really would get to France and affect the turnaround in his life that he so longed for.

Folkestone had given him nothing but grief since that first ill-fated step off the train and he wished rid of it. But Folkestone had also brought him into contact with Sally. He swirled the basinful of water with his hand as he considered whether or not he believed in fate and destiny before bending over and plunging his face into the cold water.

As his face plunged into the water for a second time, Gasmark was aware of a toilet flushing. By the time he had lifted his head and reached for the paper towel to dab himself dry, he noticed the door to one of the cubicles opening, and he froze.

Lenny, head bandaged firmly in a cap covering his entire head above the ears and a large dark pink plaster across the bridge of his nose stepped out and was greeted by the most unsuspecting surprise.

"Well, happy birthday to me," he said with an arrogant shrug of the shoulders to readjust his suit.

Gasmark simply stared at the reflection in the mirror in horror.

"Shit!" was all he managed to say before bolting for the door.

28

Gasmark exploding out of the toilet cruelly smashed the quiet, easy calm of the hospital corridor. The door swung open with such force that it smacked on the wall and bounced back.

But Gasmark was already through. He frantically grabbed the wheelchair that was sitting by the opposite wall minding its own business and pushed it back towards the door before half-falling, half-stumbling flailed off towards the lift area.

Lenny was seconds after him, but the door slammed back into his face halting his pursuit momentarily.

"Ah, fu..!" he cursed and continued straight on into the path of the wheelchair, and fell headlong onto the cold hard floor in a pile.

The frail woman in the slippers was slowly moving away from the drinks machine with four Styrofoam cups in her hands, concentrating hard on not spilling any when Gasmark careered round the corner, spotted her at the last minute and threw his body sideways, sliding less than majestically out of her way before regaining some sort of composure and carrying on down the corridor.

The woman, stunned by the sudden violent activity, focused on her drinks and was amazed that not one drop was spilt. Turning towards the lift she collided straight into the breezeblock frame of a juggernaut with a bandaged head. With nowhere else to go, her body was thrown into the air along with the four cups, which leapt higher, drink slopping out of each in wonderfully slow balletic parabolas.

"For God's sake, woman!" the juggernaut cursed, staggering back. But before she could even land on the floor, he was up and running off down the corridor.

A comfortable silence had descended on Nev and Sally as they sat beside each other and finally let the events of the previous evening sink in.

Both of them were reflecting on different aspects of the evening. Nev, whose arms were now feeling the effect of the exertion of the vans steering wheel and the rowing was reliving the manic journey through the streets of Folkestone and wondering just how he'd avoided killing himself and any number of innocent pedestrians into the bargain, while Sally was fighting an inner battle between sympathy for Rock and just letting him face up to the consequences of his nocturnal night flight.

It was Nev who broke the silence as the sound of another wheelchair being manhandled and thrown across a corridor heralded the arrival of Gasmark round the corner.

"What's up with him?"

Gasmark was upon them before anyone needed to answer.

"Lenny," he breathed, his chest on fire, "it's

Lenny..."

"What?" they both chorused.

"He...was in...the toilets."

Sally was confused. Events had suddenly taken a surreal turn for the worse.

"What's he doing here?" she asked just as Lenny roared around the corner at the far end of the corridor and bawled out loud: "GOBSHITE!" Gasmark's face blanched and he turned urgently to Sally, "I dunno, and I don't want to find out. Sal...?"

Now was not the moment to have an attack of conscience, but after all the years spent with Rock, the ups and downs, the laughs as well as the tears of absolute frustration she found herself unable to just get up and leave him.

"What about Rock?"

"He's not the only one who'll be in plaster if Lenny catches up with us," Gasmark urged, taking hold of her hand, imploring her with his eyes to come with him, "Come *on*."

Sally shook her head, "I can't. This is all my fault. I can't just leave him."

Time was running out, it was make or break. She had to make a decision and he wanted that decision to leave.

With him.

Now.

"But you already have."

"I'm sorry, Gasmark," she said softly. Then she snapped out of her melancholy and looked deep into his eyes, "Go! Before I have more hospital patients to visit."

Nev had already high-tailed it down the corridor away from the oncoming Glaswegian.

With a push from Sally Gasmark was on his way, just as Lenny thundered towards her. She had never seen him so angry. He looked as if he would tear Gasmark limb from limb if he caught him. Come to think of it he would probably do the same to her if the opportunity arose. So thinking, she ducked into the ward, and hoped for the best.

By the time Gasmark caught up with Nev he was at the main doors and together they alighted the building and stood in the car park, both puffing like decommissioned trains. But it was no time to stop.

"The van!" Gasmark urged and ran towards the van that had been parked across two parking bays earlier.

As they approached, Fowler, unshaven, still dressed in army fatigues and splattered with mud stepped out from behind the van.

"Not so fast," he said reaching into his coat and producing a tranquilizer gun.

"My God, he's got a gun!" exclaimed Nev.

Fowler waved the weapon casually, which in Gasmark's eyes made him all the dangerous. He had a manic look about him.

"I've worked it out. The midnight raids... the costumes... this Euro Poulet... It's seagulls isn't it? You've been selling contaminated seagulls. That's why their population's dropped..."

As Fowler spoke, brandishing the gun, Gasmark and Nev backed slowly around towards the van, careful not to make any sudden moves that would make an already twitchy Health Inspector squeeze the trigger.

"...which means not only have you broken the Wildlife and Countryside Act - which makes it illegal to catch or kill seagulls - and potentially poisoned half the town, but you have also attempted to make an idiot out of me... And for that, there is only one punishment."

Nev and Gasmark swallowed hard. Fowler had been squeezing the gun so tightly it suddenly jumped in his hand as it discharged a bullet-shaped dart that bounced off the van's bodywork, taking him by completely by surprise. It also had the added bonus of making the gun temporarily useless until it was reloaded.

Taking their chance, Gasmark and Nev scrambled into the front of the van. First inside, Nev slid across into the drivers' seat as another dart flew past, shattering the passenger wing mirror. Instinctively they both ducked.

"Bloody hell," said Nev, turning the key in he ignition and revving the engine, " You know how to make friends, I'll give you that!"

"Cut the funnies, Nev and just get us out of here. If Lenny catches us...well, just get us out of here!"

The van, which Nev had just slammed into reverse, shot backwards a short distance just as Lenny, pursued by a brace of Hospital Security

Guards made it to the front entrance.

"Gobshite!" he yelled, sensing yet again that Gasmark was about to slip through his fingers,

"You're a dead man!"

At the sound of Lenny's arrival, Fowler turned still waving the gun, and accidentally discharged another dart and shot Lenny in the leg.
The two Security Guards who had been chasing Lenny through the hospital halted at the sound of the shots and dived for cover, yelling into their walkie-talkies.

For his part Lenny grabbed his leg, looking down at the dart that hung on his thigh like a bee sting.

"Ow, ya fu..." he began, and turned on Fowler, but as soon as he put his weight on the tranquillized leg, it gave out from under him and he dropped to the floor in a heap.

Swerving round Lenny, Nev threw the van into first and was about to pull away when Sally appeared at a run out of the main entrance, waving for them to stop.

"Gasmark...stop!" she cried, and ran after the van.

Gasmark had seen the flash of her red cardigan out of the corner of his eye, and told Nev to stop as he climbed over he seats into the rear of the van. As the van skidded to a halt Gasmark managed to throw open the rear door in line with Sally, who took his hand and leapt up onto the van straight into his arms.

"You were right," she gasped, "I'm not going to let him hold me back any more. Let's go!"

Amidst the chaos outside the hospital, Fowler stood, tranquilizer gun limp in his hand, as the van screeched out of the hospital grounds.

Yet again his attempts had been thwarted, his plans dashed and his dreams of triumph invalidated. He saw it all tumbling down around him like a house of cards.

"No wait," he wailed at the injustice of it all, "you can't get away with this. You've broken the law... There's a penalty to... Hey! Stop!" He looked around, gun waving at his side, "Police...Security...anyone? Stop...that...van!"

For his part, Lenny had pulled himself to his feet and dragging his numbed leg, stared round wildly. A small 50cc moped swung into the front of the hospital off the main road and offered Lenny an unlikely mode of pursuit. As the moped drew to a halt, he pulled at the fluorescent high-vis jacket and in one swift motion heaved the rider off his seat before he'd had time to cut the engine.

Swinging his dead leg over the saddle, he revved the engine and took off out of the car park in the direction taken by the van. His massive frame a ridiculous sight as it sat perched upon the small bike.

Fowler, wrapped up in the ranting of the injustices and wrongdoings, was oblivious.

"They can't do that. I have official powers invested in me by the District Council," he looked about him, but no one was listening. That decided it. He would get back in his car, follow the lead of the poor sap he'd just shot, and take off after them and not give up until he'd found them and brought them in, like the bounty hunters of the Wild West.

"Right, that's it. That really is it. I will not be ignored and ridiculed any longer. I'll show them I really will, I'll show them," he was still muttering as he leapt into his Vauxhall and careered out of the car park onto the road, nearly colliding with two police cars who had been scrambled by the hospital authorities.

Instantly putting two and two together, the police cars assumed they had narrowly missed the crazed lunatic who had run amok through the hospital, and set their lights flashing as they took chase into the centre of the town.

29

Nev had no idea where he was driving to, so he just kept his eyes on the road ahead and drove. Behind them, in his rear-view mirror he could see Lenny, an elephant on a tricycle, hunched over the handlebars of a moped, occasionally waving a fist as he attempted to catch them up.

A piece of his bandage had worked itself loose and now trailed behind his head like a crepe windsock.

Behind him, swerving madly this way and that across the road, was a Vauxhall and as he checked the mirror again two police cars, blue lights flashing and sirens wailing joined the convoy. Like a shark, he had no choice but to carry on moving forwards, so he headed down towards the town centre, under Cubitt's viaduct bridge through the old town and the harbour before taking a sharp left turn and making for the Martello Towers on the cliffs.

And all the time he had one eye on the peculiar cavalcade behind him.

Fowler wasn't used to driving at speed, which accounted for the erratic nature of his pursuit. He realized that he had to keep up with the moped even if he lost sight of the van, but the motorcycle was quick and it took all his determination to match its speed. The corners began to blur and he held his breath on more than one occasion as he hit a 'sleeping policeman' with no reduction of speed.

Up ahead the vehicles dipped out of sight momentarily as the road fell away into a slope snaking down towards the harbour. Fowler stepped on his accelerator even more to increase his speed just as a motorcade of three electric mobility buggies carrying three passengers all dressed in red trundled off the pavement and onto the road directly in front of him.

Unfortunately for Fowler his first instinct was to cover his eyes, but then realized a little too late that he had taken his hands off the steering wheel.

By the time he had control of the car again it had somehow managed to avoid a collision but had veered off to the right and was bearing down on a bollard that sat defiantly in his path refusing to move. He slammed on the brakes and in a rolling cloud of burning rubber managed to slew to a halt and avoid contact.

Having been thrown forward by the emergency stop, he was now knocked back into his seat where he let out a long sigh of relief. His hands still gripped the steering wheel so tightly his knuckles had turned white, and his wrists screamed their pain. Fowler stared dead ahead. "Arse!" he yelled out in sheer frustration.

"I've fackin' got yer now," Lenny thought as Nev's directionless flight took him up away from the town and towards the Martello Tower and the cliffs. Sure enough, as the van departed from the road and headed across the grass towards the edge of the cliff, it naturally slowed. Whereas Lenny, perched atop the 50cc moped coped much better with the surface, and he realized that he had them; there was nowhere left to run.

Yet still the van continued valiantly bumping and kangarooing over the rough ground as Nev continued to fight the steering wheels worst instincts.

Gasmark, alerted by the sudden change in road surface looked through to the drivers cabin.

"What are you doing? Look out!" he screamed as the cliff edge came closer and closer with every bone-crunching bump but it was no good, there was too much kinetic energy to prevent the inevitable and Nev decided to it was time to admit defeat.

"Woaaaah!" he yelled, "Jump!"

Lenny saw the cliff edge rising up, and was then aware of doors being flung open and the passengers all tumbling out of the back of the van while Nev leapt from the drivers' door. All landed with maximum indignity on the rough tufted grass before rolling over and over until they came to a stop just in time to watch the van continues on its journey towards oblivion.

As it reached the edge of the cliff the van jumped a little into the air as the ground below its front wheel fell away. The further into thin air it reached the more violently it twisted to the left and began its inextricable descent.

For Nev, Gasmark and Sally it was the end of the line. Their luck had run out, and so, inevitably, had their road. They got to their feet slowly, checking for broken bones.

"That was close," said Nev.

Horry gazed about him with no clue as to what had really just happened. In the past few hours he had been set upon by youths, sought solace in the strongest cider he could afford, nearly drowned and been thrown out of a moving van. All he wanted was an explanation.

"Could someone tell me what exactly is going on?" he asked as the sounds of crunching metal were heard coming up from the bottom of the cliff.

The van had landed.

"My van!" Gasmark moaned, "You've trashed my van!"

"Relax, you're insured," Nev replied, "aren't you?"

"I hope that includes medical cover," Sally added as Lenny's moped came to a halt and he jumped off, still hobbling with his numbed leg and set chase in a blaze of obscenities.

For a fleeting moment Gasmark felt that it was not just the van that would end up over the cliff. Faced with that prospect or a chase, he turned on his heel and made for the Martello Tower.

Behind him Lenny, ignoring the others, set off

in dogged pursuit, dragging his incapacitate leg behind. It slowed him down but he wasn't going to give up. His grievance was personal and now, upon this chalk cliff-top, it had come down to the two of them - a final face-off of cinematic scope.

In his minds eye he could see the crane shot as it swooped across the two of them, coming to rest further up he cliff for their ultimate showdown.

He could almost hear the John Williams score building to a crescendo of brass and strings as the narrative reached its gripping conclusion.

"Gobshite!" he yelled at the retreating figure up ahead, "Gobshite, ye bastard. Come here!"

Although he was some way off, Lenny got the impression he was gaining, that Gasmark was flagging terminally. Infact it looked as though he was stopping.

"Lenny," he shouted back between great gulps of air, "Lenny, I can explain. It's not how it looks, honest!"

"We'll see about that," he growled through his gritted teeth, pushing on, beyond reasoning. Every step, every heavy drag of his paralyzed leg brought him closer. Gasmark was running, stumbling and tripping into a dead-end. Lenny grinned at the word, never before had it been more apposite.

Then suddenly he had his first real stroke of luck. Up ahead Gasmark, a mess of arms and legs went over in spectacular fashion. He had been running so fast and so uncoordinatedly that his body gave up trying to work out which arm or leg should be going forward or back and just sent him flying close to the edge of the cliff.

In an instant, Lenny was upon him, pulling him up by the lapels.

"Be reasonable," he begged as Lenny bore down on him, breathing hard.

"Reasonable?" As he spoke, white frothy bubbles of spittle formed at the side of his mouth and spattered over Gasmark's face.

"Reasonable's no' in my vocabulary. Reasonable's no' even been INVENTED! You ken wha' I'm sayin'? You took the piss, now you're gonna pay."

With one violent movement Lenny pulled his bandaged head back and brought his forehead down hard on the bridge of Gasmark's nose in a swift head-butt.

"Stitch that!" he said and let go of the jacket. Another lightning bolt flashed across Gasmark's eyes. Pain flooded his head as he dropped to the floor, holding his nose. Blood squirted out of the cut and bubbled over his hands.

"Oh my God, he's going to kill him!" Sally screamed. Together with Nev and Horry they had followed Lenny up onto the cliff-top and now stood helpless as the towering Glaswegian caught up with and began meting out his punishment.

"Gasmark!" He looked up at the sound of Sally's voice as he staggered to his feet holding his bloodied nose. In the dizzying confusion that enveloped his head, Gasmark stepped sideways;

his one focused thought was keeping away from the cliff edge and out of reach of Lenny's balled fists. Like the prize fighter he'd always wanted to be, Lenny watched as Gasmark wobbled to the right. Instinctively he moved round readying for his next punch. He stood back and without thinking shifted his weight onto his numbed leg and felt the whole of his world buckle as he stumbled and lost his footing.

"Whoa? God. Shite!" he said clawing the air. He managed to grab hold of Gasmark's T-Shirt and hung on as he tried to regain his balance on the precipice.

"For the lath-t time," said Gasmark, coming out of the pain and seizing the moment, "MY...NAME...ITH...GATHMARK!" and whipped his hand up so quickly that Lenny let go and instantly lost his balance.

In one last attempt at self-preservation he flapped his arms and was aware of three seagulls that had risen up on the thermals thrown up by the cliff. They hung in the air, riding the wind currents mocking his attempts. As he felt himself pitch backwards he looked at Gasmark and his eyes widened.

For the first time he knew fear
"Whoa. Oh. Ohhhhhhhhh...."

Both his arms windmilled but to no avail and he disappeared out of sight.

The moment of triumph and relief rested on Gasmark's shoulders for a split second. As Lenny dropped a last, desperate hand grabbed his ankle and pulled him off the edge.

Sally's hands flew up to her face as she saw her lover disappear off the cliff edge.

"Gasmark!" she screamed and, along with Horry and Nev, ran to the edge and looked over.

Far below the large and familiar frame of Lenny could be seen lying twisted and bent in the van. He had plummeted right through the roof leaving a huge hole. But there was no sign of Gasmark in amongst the debris.

"GASMARK!" she cried, fearing the absolute worst, not expecting an answer. Just when it had seemed that they were about to be free of Lenny and his extortionate interest rates and threatening presence he had, with a final action, taken away her newly discovered hope for the future. She turned away, unable to bear the loss.

"Down here!" a voice called up. A familiar voice, slightly nasal and suffering the effects of congealing blood, but one only a moment ago she thought she would never hear again.

She looked back over the edge and to her joy saw Gasmark clinging to a small lip about five feet below the cliff edge.

"Gasmark!" she shouted down, relief engulfing her, " Thank God! I thought I'd lost you!"

Common sense and practicality, Sally's two watchwords came to bear on the situation. She got down on her knees and realised that Gasmark was too far from the edge of the cliff to just be able to pull him up so she lay on the grass and instructed Horry and Nev to take a leg each and ease her over the edge so that Gasmark could reach up and pull himself to safety.

"Gimme your hand!" she urged, stretching her arms out as far as she could. Gasmark had a precarious hold on the lip of rock and was reluctant to move, even in the slightest.

"I can't."

Sally summoned up her reserves and forced herself to stretch a few tantalizing inches further. Seeing her effort, and the look on her face, he tentatively let go of the rock with his right hand and edged it close and closer towards her outstretched fingertips.

"Come...on!" she urged. Her fingertips wiggled, but they would not reach him. There was nothing else she could do; it was all up to him now.

He lifted his leg and felt around for a foothold, some dent or gap in the rock face that he could put his boot into and lever himself up just a fraction to reach Sally's straining outstretched hand. He found a recess and dug the toe of his boot in and pushed down, only to feel the chalk crumble away beneath him. As the tiny rock fragments fell away to the ground below he turned his head.

"Don't look down!" Sally yelled too late. He'd looked down and beneath him the earth spun. The cliff telescoped away from him, the crumpled roof of the van beckoned and the stirring figure of Lenny a stark reminder of where he would end up if he didn't pull his finger out.

He forced himself to look away and up towards Sally. Towards his future and beyond. All he needed to do was climb.

With a determined push his foot found another hold and he pushed. This time the rock held and he found himself rising higher. His fingertips touched Sally's and kept going until he was able to grab hold of her hand, and he was ready for rescue.

"Pull!" he shouted.

30

Fowler was inconsolable. Somehow he had managed not only to lose the van he'd so doggedly pursued, but also his way and now stared unblinkingly at a dead end at the foot of the cliff. There was nothing ahead of him except large chucks of rock that had clearly becoming dislodged from the cliff higher up and fallen to the ground where they had either smashed into smaller pieces or just remained as one larger mass.

Whichever way he looked at it though, he was lost. Opening the door of the Vauxhall he stepped out onto the rough ground and stared up at the high cliff that seemed to sway. Slowly he moved away from the car and kicked some of the pebble-sized stones totally disconsolate and at the end of his tether.

"No, not again! I had them in my sights, I was this close." He raved aloud to the silent rocks, holding up his thumb and forefinger an inch apart, "Where did I go wrong?"

Suddenly, as if in answer from above, there was the metallic sound of something bouncing off rock. As he looked up at the cliffs edge the van had begun its relentless and inevitable journey down. It collided with rocks that jutted out, it broke them off and they showered down onto the ground, and it bounced a little further away from the rock face until it entered its final descent path and landed firmly and squarely with a deadening crunch right on top of the Vauxhall, crushing it flat.

This was the last straw - the final insult. At the sight of his car now resting flatly under the van whose wheels were now just spinning to a stop, Fowler felt the rise of impotent rage and gave way to hysteria.

His heaving sobs and wailing cries of self-pity were interrupted minutes later by another voice which began high up and far away and grew rapidly louder and nearer and sounded, to Fowler, like "Gobshiiiiiiite!"

Picking his head up from the cradle of his hands he was just in time to see the stranger he had shot with the tranquilizer gun in his last moments of free flight before coming to a sudden, and noisy landing at the end of a fall that was broken by the roof of the van now sitting on his car.

It was all too much for him. Reason had been stripped from him and the arms of madness; wonderful uncluttered madness opened up and beckoned him forwards.

He was almost relieved when he saw the blue lights of the police squad car followed by an ambulance approaching.

When people go flying off cliff tops one can generally rely on a witness with a mobile phone to alert the emergency services, and so it was that Fowler was saved. Once they had drawn up, he was helped, jabbering, into the back of the police car and driven away.

Behind him the paramedics climbed into the wreck of the van to find Lenny broken but not bowed. Because of his constitution, he had not, unlike Fowler's car, been written off, and as he was stretchered out of the van he stared wild-eyed and crazy up at the cliff edge.

"I'll get you Gobshite!" he called out spitting blood and rabid saliva, "You're a dead man! Hear me? A DEAD MAN!" over and over again as he was lifted into the back of the ambulance.

31

After its long, hot stay the summer was finally ready to leave. It had rolled up its towels, taken in its parasols and packed its bags and now stood on the edge of the season.

Gasmark stood on the deck of the cross-channel ferry as it pulled out of Dover harbour and into open water looking decidedly unwell. His cheeks were pallid with a distinct touch of green. His hair flew about in the sturdy breeze and he breathed in long and deep in an attempt to shift the nausea. The sickly mix of diesel and brine that filled his nostrils only reinforced his desire to gag. Feeling his stomach spasm again he leaned over the rail and retched.

Sally returned with two bottles of water to the sight of him bent double.

"How are you feeling now?" she asked above the wind.

"Like I'm gonna be sick." He turned away from the handrail and came to sit besides Sally who was popping a Kwells travel sickness tablet out of a blister pack and handing it to him along with the bottle of water. Gasmark took the pill and a mouthful of water.

"Thanks. You sure this is a good idea?" Sally was reading the packet, "Of course, it says *'should be taken around thirty minutes before travel, however can also be taken once a journey has started if you begin to feel sick'*."

"I meant us and France."

"It's what you've always wanted, isn't it?" she asked, slipping the box of tablets into her bag,

"So now the insurance company's paid up, you've got no excuses. Remember what Horry used to say: 'Just jump in and do it'?"

"I was talking about Rock," he said, casting shade over the conversation. There was no avoiding it, a little part of him still felt like a heel, and he would be lying if he didn't think Sally probably did too, "What would he think, me flying off with his bird?"

The wind cut in and she turned her face against it, remembering the last time she had seen him.

Before leaving for France she had gone to the hospital with the intention of putting things straight. To close the door with a click not with a slam.

The flowers she had brought suddenly felt wrong as she looked in through a glass window at Rock, sitting immobile in a wheelchair wearing a stiff-neck collar, legs in plaster and both arms set in 'broom handle' plaster casts; a cruel parody of a pair of wings.

He was gazing out of the window at a flurry of seagulls, his dream of flight over and suddenly she didn't know why she had come, she felt nothing for him, not even pity. Here was a man she didn't recognize. She was about to leave when Lexxie appeared behind her.

"I think we've lost him," she said

enigmatically. Sally looked at her and handed over the flowers.

"I don't think so," she said, "It's just a case of being there when he lands", and had walked away.

"He made his choice when he jumped off that roof," she announced returning to the present,

"And I've made mine. Look." She reached out and took Gasmark's hand and together they looked at the Ferries' wake, snaking away white towards the fast shrinking harbour wall where, staring out into the Channel, stood Horry with a toy telescope he'd found sticking out of a bin. He had insisted on seeing them off, and as he saw them wave he stiffened and shot his right arm up in a naval salute.

"Always keep your eyes on the horizon!" he shouted into the wind.

While Gasmark and Sally sat on the ferry deck watching the coast of England slowly disappear from view, Nev was busy with his camera around the ferry collecting wild track footage of the other passengers, the sky, the coast, the seagulls as they hung in the air.

When they had told him of their plans he had immediately suggested he join them. Lenny's injuries would heal eventually, he'd argued, and then he would come after them and Nev didn't fancy being the one left behind to face whatever music Lenny chose to play.

"The funeral business is dying on its arse,"

he'd reasoned, "whereas France...well, it's not just great food, mate, the films ain't so bad either. I could relaunch the whole *Nouvelle Vague* thing...I got all the kit. There's nothing for me in Folkestone, not with you two going."

He'd been so relentlessly persuasive, that in the end both Sally and Gasmark reckoned, like the three musketeers, they had been through a lot together and it would be fun to share the adventure with each other.

Presently Nev returned to the deck with his camera, smiling broadly. Clearly the filming had gone well.

"This is great!" he bubbled with enthusiasm, "I shoulda done this years ago. Forget funerals, this is the business. I can see it now: *Un film de Neville Bell*. All I need is a catchy title."

"How about '*Gregory's Gull*'?" Gasmark suggested. The nausea had begun to wear off as the Kwells calmed his stomach and he felt well enough to indulge Nev in some word play. For his part, Nev switched the camera back on and framed Gasmark to the left of the shot before panning right to catch Sally.

"Yeah, yeah, or... or '*Gullipoli*'?" They both shared the laugh.

"No, no, wait. I got it, I got it," Gasmark exclaimed getting to his feet and spreading his arms wide as he broke into song: "*Gull-dfinger*," he begun before Sally leapt up to chorus: "He's the bird, the bird with the Midas touch!"

Nev crabbed around them as they sang, urging them to continue, "Yeah yeah yeah. Keep it going. This is great, very in the moment! Oh, they're gonna *love* this in Cannes."

Their laughter trailed round them as they sang, disturbed only by a solitary seagull who swooped down and around them, joining in with its all-too-familiar call sounding, as it always had to Gasmark, like Tarzan's jungle call on helium.

Nev zoomed in on the bird with a smile on his face.

"Anyone for lunch?" he asked.

- END –

Coming soon, the follow-up to *"Seagulls On Speed"*:

"The Grapes of Ralph"

When Gasmark's relative leaves him a cardboard box of oddities and keepsakes in her will he has no idea that it will change his life forever.
The only trouble is, he's stuck in France bemoaning the fact that his Contentantal dream has turned into something of a nightmare.
Meanwhile, Nev is caught making some rather dodgy videos featuring some scantily clad women and Sally realises that a full-time career job is not all it's cracked up to be.
Could it be time to return to England and see exactly what's in the box?

Grapes of Ralph © 2017 Graeme Scarfe

AFTERWORD:
Some notes on the saga of Seagulls On Speed.

This has been a long journey. *Seagulls On Speed* was a film script before it became a book; and before that it was an idea born out of a snappy title floating around my head when I lived and wrote in Folkestone.

By the time I got round to writing the initial screenplay for *Seagulls On Speed* a few years later I had three very precise castings in mind. It always helps if I have the perfect casting (even if its in my own head) when writing. First, Paul Reynolds, an actor I'd admired since I saw him in the TV show *Press Gang*. I loved his comic timing and his onscreen persona and knew that he would bring to all that to the part of Nev.

Then there was Fish as Lenny. Fish had been frontman with rock band Marillion whom I adored from the first moment I heard them in 1983. Apart from his career as a singer-songwriter he has also acted on TV and Film, notably *'Young Person's Guide to Being a Rock Star'*. When Lenny appeared on the first page totally out-of-the blue (the character wasn't even in the step outline) he was a tall, bald Scotsman. Who else would I want to cast but Fish?

Finally I always wanted John Otway to play Horry. I'd first seen him perform at the Theatre Royal, Bury St. Edmunds in the very early 1980s and had been a fan of long standing. We exchanged e-mails, met a few times in Brighton and casting agreed (I was by that time associate producer on the project and was trying to get the bird to fly).

Knowing he'd recorded the title song for the feature version of *'Whoops! Apocalypse'* I also suggested he write the theme tune to run under the end credits of the proposed film. Anyway, one thing led to another and the finances fell through. The seagull was a dodo dead in the water.

Years later, frustrated with the state of the British film industry I wrote the book just to get it out there.

Fast forward over a decade later, just after Christmas 2016 and an e-mail arrived from John. He'd been working on a new album and *'Seagulls On Speed'*, the song he'd written but never told me about, had been recorded and was going to be on it. To say I'm thrilled and honored is a massive understatement.

If you're interested in hearing the song that was inspired by the screenplay that was inspired by a throwaway title, you can find the track on *Montserrat* by John Otway available through www.johnotway.com

Someday, somewhere, someone might pick up the book and think it would make a good film or television series, and if so...CONTACT MY AGENT! But until then here's the book and the song it inspired. What more could a writer want?